Classic
SCOOTERS

Classic SCOOTERS

Mike Webster

p

Page 1: Zündapp Bella 200. The last version of this fine German tourer.

Page 2: Lightweight simplicity from France meets heavyweight luxury from Germany. 115cc Mors Speed (1951) and 197cc TWN Contessa (1956).

Page 3: Rumi Bol d'Or. A production high performance Rumi made to celebrate race successes in the famous 24-hour motorcycle races. Only available in gold/white and very desirable.

This is a Parragon book
This edition published in 2004

Copyright © Parragon 1997

Parragon
Queen Street House
4 Queen Street
Bath BA1 1HE, UK

Designed, produced and packaged by
Stonecastle Graphics Ltd

Edited by Philip de Ste. Croix

ISBN 1-40544-337-5

Printed in Indonesia

Photographic credits
The publishers would like to thank the following for permission to reproduce their photographs:
National Motor Museum Pages 15 and 19.
Imperial War Museum Pages 9 and 21.
Classic Bike Magazine Pages 47 and 60.
All other pictures by Mike Webster and kindly supplied by friends and scooter organizations.

Figures and data in this book are quoted in metric measurements first, with the Imperial equivalents noted in brackets.

Acknowledgements:
The author gratefully acknowledges the assistance given by the following friends and organizations without which this book could not have been created; Colin Bathe, Martin Brench, Mike Dann, Bill Dorling, Bill Drake, Graham Fisher, Sarah Green, Ian Harrop, Matthias Henze, Phil Hingston, the Imperial War Museum, Italjet SpA, Wynford Jones, Gail Lake, Stuart Lanning, Len Melling, the National Motor Museum, the Science Museum, New Scootering Magazine, Mark Summers, the Vintage Scooter Club, David Walker, Michael Ware and, in particular, Valerie Humble for her patience in typing and altering the text. Thanks to all other friends who have offered help, encouragement and the loan of photographs for possible inclusion.

Contents

Introduction

THE TITLE of this book is not intended to be contentious. It is not easy to define a scooter let alone a 'classic' scooter. This book is intended to interest and give pleasure to its readers through text and pictures. It makes no claims to being a definitive, nor indeed exhaustive, chronicle of such machines.

The term scooter as applied to motorized transport has a very wide application. To many, scooters conjure up a picture of small wheeled, lightweight and brightly coloured economical transport, specifically designed for the non-mechanically minded. For most of us it is common knowledge that scooters were sold in vast quantities in the post- Second World War period until, the availability of small inexpensive cars and increasing consumer affluence caused a down turn in their popularity.

Above: Early French luxury. The 1953 Bernardet came with leather fringed saddle/panniers, windscreen and spare wheel.

Left: The 1958 Vespa GS 150 and 1963 Lambretta TV175 are representative of the 'classic scooter' at it's best.

Throughout the quarter century from 1950, scooter sales were dominated by two Italian companies (Piaggio and Innocenti) who sold their Vespa and Lambrettas scooters in such vast quantities that they were the envy of every motorcycle manufacturer throughout the world.

A phenomenal culture was spawned by the post-war popularity of scooters with social clubs, sporting, leisure events and fashions all stemming from the ownership of them.

Left: Differing solutions to a common need in 1956. The 125cc cigar shaped Piatti marketed for lady owners meets heavyweight German luxury in the TWN Contessa.

Whilst the majority of scooter sales were made in two decades, the whole picture is much wider and spans more than 80 years.

This book features scooters from around the world, the story beginning in the early nineteen hundreds and ending with speculation on what may form the basis of future classics.

All the machines included in this book are scooters, although some diverge from the conventional image with motorcycle style wheels or unenclosed components.

Like scooters, the word 'Classic' is equally difficult to define. The machines included are here because they are collected zealously by an ever-growing group of scooter enthusiasts. Many feature innovative construction or (for their time) advanced ideas.

Above: The author, pictured here earning his Gold Medal in the Isle of Man Scooter Week of 1976 on a Moto Rumi. Events included sprinting, regularity trials and enduros.

Left: The Italjet Formula 125 is late 1990s state-of-the art with a twin cylinder 125cc motor and trick suspension. Machines like this are probably the classic scooters of the future.

Scooter Origins

THE MOTOR scooter has its roots in the public need for inexpensive personal mobility. Whilst two World Wars have had terrible and often unjustifiable consequences, a positive outcome of such conflicts was the consequent rapid advances in technology. During the First World War, military engineering underwent major expansion and at the end of hostilities, there were many companies without military work and with spare manufacturing capacity. Unsurprisingly, several of these businesses looked at the field of personal transport and several manufacturers sprung up offering sometimes innovative and occasionally diabolical devices under the name of scooters.

This first generation of scooters never sold in large quantities and with one or two exceptions, this

Above: Was this 1894 Hildebrand and Wolfmueller the first scooter? An open frame and small wheel are both evident.

is probably just as well! The machines of this generation included in this book offered widely differing engineering solutions to a post-war need for mobility and, unfettered by convention or previous experience, introduced some of the enduring characteristics that differentiate scooters from motorcycles. Whilst most motorcycles have evolved around one basic configuration, scooter designers often started with a blank sheet of paper creating an exciting variety of design and unusual or innovative construction.

The first generation of scooters enjoyed a brief popularity but had effectively died out by the mid-1920s. It was not until the Second World War that they reappeared primarily for military use. English, German, Italian and American

Left: The 269cc Reynolds Runabout was available with chain or belt drive and offered excellent weather protection.

Above: The ancestor to the Vespa! Piaggio made 100 of these 1945 scooters before the Vespa was launched in 1946.

manufacturers all produced simple scooters to mobilize parachute regiments and ground forces. Again, the solutions were varied – perhaps the most famous being the British Welbike which folded and was dropped by parachute inside a canister alongside the troops. America had the Cushman, Germany the TWN and Italy had twin wheels at each end of their Volugrafo.

Immediately after the Second World War, everybody wanted to get mobile again and most of the engineering companies which had been kept busy with war work had spare capacity. The result was a proliferation of second generation scooters.

Italian aircraft makers, Piaggio, were not allowed to continue making aeroplanes and so instead, in 1945, they created a small monocoque scooter. After producing only 100 or so of these little machines, a new model called the Vespa (Wasp) was launched. This machine was so advanced that its shape and engineering principles formed the basis of all the Vespa scooters sold up to the mid-1990s. Originally of 98cc capacity, it evolved through 125cc, 150cc and later 200cc.

Engineering giant Innocenti from Milan launched its transport for the masses in 1947 with the Lambretta M (later renamed the Model A). Unlike the Vespa, the Lambretta was open-framed with tubular construction and it did not offer much weather protection. The first Lambretta had no suspension and thus relied on its balloon tyres to absorb the bumps. This was soon replaced with the model B (an A with proper sprung suspension). From this point on, the Lambretta and Vespa vied for market share and developed bigger and better machines. For the most part, Lambretta stayed true to its tubular frame origins with either shaft- or totally enclosed chain-drive. whilst Vespa never deviated from it's concept of a monocoque body shell with the engine/gear box unit mounted inside/adjacent to the rear wheel.

Below: The British Welbike was dropped by parachute in a cylindrical container as mobility for WWII troops.

A rivalry grew between these two products that was as intensely felt by their customers as it was by the marketing men. Even today, scooter riders are passionately divided into Vespa or Lambretta camps but rarely both!

In the early 1950s sales of Vespa and Lambretta took off in a way that no two-wheeler sales had ever done. Very quickly almost every motorcycle manufacturer, cycle maker and engineering shop was scurrying to capture market share. Some of their products displayed abysmal styling and engineering; others totally lost the basic scooter concept of simple economical transport and produced larger, ever more sophisticated and luxurious mounts.

The market could not adequately support the sudden flood of such diverse machines and many were short-lived. Although some were excellent, the market was over-supplied with a confusion of models. The result was that even many of the good designs (with the exception of the two dominant market leaders) could not truly succeed. Too little, too late was to be their fate.

If 'classic' simply meant quantity, then this book would be full of Lambrettas and Vespas. The truth is that a number of the largely unknown, low-volume scooters were well engineered, high quality, innovative machines. The variety of engineering solutions is testimony to individualistic engineers and talented designers far removed from the computer-aided design of the virtually identical offerings of the 1990s.

Sadly for the scooter, inexpensive small cars like the Fiat 500 and the Mini soon enticed an ever more prosperous consumer base away from the rain, cold and relative lack of protection afforded by

Above: A 1946 Vespa. It had a 98cc motor and no stand. Parking involved leaning the footboard against a kerb.

Right: These workers were to find scooter production kept them employed when World War II ended.

two-wheel travel. By the mid-1960s, scooter sales were in serious decline, supported only by the sub-cultures and fashions that had grown up among the scooter clubs they had spawned.

By the 1990s we were left with a handful of European scooters. Only now are the Japanese, French and Italians establishing a third generation based more on style and image that the need for utility transport. High-tech engineering and materials linked with outrageous colour schemes are needed to entice the young and not-so-poor to purchase the latest offerings. Pop stars and sporting personalities have adopted the third generation scooters as trendy and trick transport. With such people as role models, the young are, once again, buying scooters in increasing numbers. In years to come, it will be interesting to see which of the present exotica will achieve classic status.

Left: Jon Elison of Cheltenham Vespa Club braves the giant see-saw at a scooter rally in Neuss, Germany.

Above: This Lambretta LD150 sports some of the wide range of accessories available to personalize scooters.

Autoped

THE AUTOPED was first patented on 19 May 1915. The original design was referred to as the Marks Motorscooter. The patent credits the Auto-Ped Company of 569 Fifth Avenue, Manhattan, New York with the design on 26th of January of that year. The description in the patent application is as follows: 'The front motor and steering wheel is arranged in tandem with the rear wheel and the rider stands on a platform disposed preferably below the wheel centres and holds a stabilising bar hinged at its lower end to the steering head. The bar being then in an approximately vertical position may form a petrol tank with the hinged joint allowing petrol to flow to the engine when the bar is upright but shutting off the petrol when the bar is folded down. The crankshaft of the motor is arranged co-axially with the steering wheel and drives the wheel through reducing epicyclical gears. A brakeband can be expanded so as to engage the inside of the front wheel, this band being operated by rearward movements of the stabilising bar.'

From this patent was derived the American Ever-Ready Autoped which, for many people, represents the beginning of the motorscooter.

The design closely followed that of a child's push scooter. In line with the original patent, the Autoped had no seat – the rider had to stand and move the steering column (forwards engaged the drive and rearward disengaged the clutch and applied the front brake).

One change from the original patent was the abandonment of the proposed use of the steering column as a fuel tank. Production Autopeds had a small fuel tank mounted above the front mudguard.

Left: It is easy to see from this angle why motoring writers of the day mistakenly thought and reported that the Autoped was battery powered.

WOULDN'T YOU LIKE TO "SCOOT" WITH ME ?

"DE LA VIE PARISIENNE"

« C'EST LA MODE NOUVELLE MADEMOISELLE !.... »

Above: The innovative Autoped even captured the imagination of post card artists, as seen in these examples from 1920.

Despite the dubious practicality of such a vehicle, the Autoped was made under licence in the United Kingdom and Germany (known as the Krupp).

This Autoped weighs 43.5kg (96lb), 35 of which are on the front wheel. The motor is a single cylinder unit of 155cc using an automatic inlet valve and a mechanically operated exhaust valve. The unit is mounted on the left-hand side and on the same axis as the front wheel which is driven through a back gear and clutch. The final drive ratio is 5.2 : 1 and the clutch is engaged when the column is pushed fully forward. In the mid-position, the steering column disengages the drive and the machine will freewheel, whilst pulling it back will apply the front brake. There is no rear brake.

Amusingly, several contemporary journalists described the Autoped as an electric scooter due to it being termed the Ever-Ready Autoped. Ever-Ready, in the UK at least, made batteries and the large box on the legshield, which simply served as a storage unit, was apparently mistaken for one!

Construction of the machine is unusual in that the frame and front forks are formed out of sheet steel pressings and plates rather than conventional tubing. The only tubes in the construction are those of the steering column and handlebars. The pressed-steel disc wheels are fitted with red pneumatic tyres also made by Autoped. In America and the UK, some users actually attempted to race their Autopeds!

Original road tests of the period described the Autoped as 'a handy, single-track automobile for runabout use. Continuous journeys of up to 16 kilometres (10 miles) can be made without fatigue under ordinary road conditions'. The article also described the Autoped as suitable for use in situations that would be impossible for an orthodox motorcycle to cope with but unfortunately it did not describe specifically what these were.

In 1919 one road test stated that 'the steadiness and cleanliness of the machine, under adverse weather conditions, left nothing to be desired' and that 'the machine was considered the most usable and manufacturable design so far produced'. Maximum speed was in the region of 16km/h (10mph).

The American Ever-Ready Autoped was truly an unique approach to personal transport, pre-dating other production scooters by a number of years.

Left: The 1916 Autoped was ridden from a standing position. The steering column pivots forward to engage the drive and when pulled back, disengages the motor and applies the brake. For storage, the column folds and attaches to the rear mudguard.

13

SPECIFICATION: AUTOPED	
YEAR	1916
CUBIC CAPACITY	155cc
BORE	56mm
STROKE	63mm
COMPRESSION RATIO	N/A
POWER	N/A
TOP SPEED	16km/h (10mph)
UK PRICE	£20

ABC *Skootamota*

THE SKOOTAMOTA was undoubtedly one of the best products to emerge from the first generation of scooters. The designer and creator was Granville Bradshaw, who is perhaps better known for his remarkable 400cc flat twin motorcycle.

The ABC scooter which first appeared in 1919, consists of a low platform with a pedestal seat at one end and tall handlebars at the other. The power unit is a very compact, horizontal, single cylinder, petrol engine mounted over the rear wheel and controlled by just two levers on the handlebars. There are no gears and the speed range from the 125cc overhead-inlet, side-exhaust valve motor is variable between 3km/h (2mph) and 24km/h

Above: A Christmas card from 1923 clearly inspired by the interesting Skootamota design of Granville Bradshaw.

Left: The compact horizontal motor sits above the rear wheel with the air cooled single cylinder pointing to the rear. A reduction geared chain drives the rear wheel.

(15mph). Sales brochures of the day described this range as spanning less than walking pace to faster than a trotting horse. In 1919, road tests reported that the Skootamota was capable of negotiating any ordinary main road hill even with a heavy rider, and that it had climbed two-thirds of the way up the infamous Brooklands Test Hill. It was also described as very comfortable to ride, very easy to manage, and requiring no mechanical knowledge at all to own.

14

SPECIFICATION: ABC SKOOTAMOTA	
YEAR	1919
CUBIC CAPACITY	125cc
BORE	60mm
STROKE	44mm
COMPRESSION RATIO	N/A
POWER	N/A
TOP SPEED	24km/h (15mph)
PRICE UK	£40

The frame consists mainly of four small diameter tubes with triangulation and cross-bracing to form a lightweight but rigid structure. The wheels are 40.6cm (16in) in diameter with external contracting brakes, front and rear. A magneto mounted opposite the rear-facing cylinder feeds the sparking plug whilst the fuel and oil tank are mounted immediately above the motor.

The Skootamota probably sold more examples than all other first-generation scooters put together, proving, perhaps, that in its short production run between 1919 and 1923 the public were discerning enough to recognize a practical value-for-money package.

The name ABC incidentally stands for All British Cycle and reflected the patriotic view of the period that Britain was the leader in world motorcycling.

Above: The ABC Skootamota is one of the most practical early scooter designs with clever use made of small diameter tubes for its lightweight frame. With its overhead inlet and side exhaust valves, the motor gives a good performance up to 24km/h (15mph).

Unibus

THE UNIBUS has the distinction of being the first totally enclosed scooter with a design that looks more in keeping with the 1950s than its 1920 origin.

Prior to the Unibus, all early scooters were open-framed, and for the most part, of little practicality. The Unibus was designed by Harold Boultebee and anticipated the general configuration that we all expect of the motor scooter by more than quarter of a century.

Contemporary advertisements described the Unibus as 'a car on two wheels'. It is worth

Below: Seat removal reveals a large storage locker, and a hand crank inside the legshield starts the motor.

remembering that in 1920, weather protection in most cars was poor, so perhaps the description was not misleading. Here, however, is perhaps the first clue to its lack of sales success. The UK asking price of £75 would actually buy a motor car. In addition, other scooters offered just prior to the unveiling of the Unibus had been the subject of criticism by the established motorcycle press. Against this background, the Unibus was never going to find many buyers.

At first glance, the Unibus appears unremarkable, but only because many of its features are commonplace in modern scooters. The motorcycle press stated that it was a world apart from the crop of flimsy alternatives. The 'car on two wheels' description goes further than describing the all-enveloping bodywork, as the construction of the Unibus is based on a pressed-steel car-type chassis (very advanced for 1920) whilst a starting handle inside the leg shield works exactly like that fitted to motor cars of the period.

Technically, the Unibus was generally 40 years ahead of its time. In the 1960s Velocette copied the front engine shaft drive and rear wheel-mounted gearbox arrangement for their highly praised Viceroy scooter.

The two-stroke engine is mounted directly behind the front wheel with a single dry-plate clutch and propeller shaft running into a two-speed gearbox mounted in the rear wheel. This arrangement gives an excellent weight distribution for the whole scooter.

Cooling air reaches the motor via a large grille on the front apron and under the high cutaway front mudguard. This air passes round the fins of the vertical cylinder and exits via two slots on the rear edge of the leg shield. The starting handle is connected to the crank-shaft via two sprockets and a chain.

Unusually, the Unibus has quarter elliptical leaf springing front and rear. Most scooters and motorcycles of the period offer little or no suspension. Two sets of internally expanding brake shoes operate on the rear wheel. One set is activated by a handlebar lever and the second by the rider's left heel. (Most brakes in the 1920s were of the external contracting type, demonstrating yet again the advanced engineering of the Unibus that we now take for granted.)

Immediately above the motor are the fuel tank and oil tank. Lubrication is via a drip-feed sight glass with a vernier to adjust the amount of oil entering the motor. This principle of separate petrol and oil feed was widely copied 40 years later and is now the norm for modern two-strokes.

With two gears, a top speed of 40km/h (26mph) is possible from the Unibus. The gear ratios are 6 : 1 and 10 : 1.

The list of innovations goes on: split-rim disc wheels were available and a large storage area was contained under the seat. Electric lighting was offered as an accessory fed from a dry battery mounted in the storage area. Pump, tools and several small parcels could all be easily accommodated.

The Unibus as the first totally enclosed scooter, has most of the features that we all take for granted in modern machines. It must be considered as the true forerunner of all modern scooters with a quality of construction achieved by it's makers, the Gloucestershire Aircraft Company, in keeping with its technical superiority and high price.

Below: A technical marvel with quarter-elliptical spring suspension (front/rear) and shaft drive. The body was also a first and looks like it could have been designed 30 years later.

Above: The brochure reflects the Unibus' high price and superior quality. Colour printing was unusual in 1920.

SPECIFICATION: UNIBUS	
YEAR	1920
CUBIC CAPACITY	269cc
BORE	70mm
STROKE	70mm
COMPRESSION RATIO	N/A
POWER	N/A
TOP SPEED	40km/h (25mph)
PRICE UK	£75

Autoglider

ALTHOUGH SOME of the early scooters were candidly hopeless, the Autoglider was a serious attempt to provide useful mobility.

The designer was Charles R. Townsend, who owned the Townsend Engineering Company in Birmingham. The first Autoglider was constructed in 1919. The prototype, like many scooters of the period, was ridden in a standing position and powered by a 269cc Villiers engine driving the front wheel. The production Model A that followed changed little, although the wheel size was increased from 30.5cm (12in) to 40.6cm (16in) and the Villiers engine was replaced with a Union motor (from a company that still exists today making locks and padlocks) and increased in size to 292cc.

Charles Townsend was strong on marketing skills and organized a number of publicity stunts to stimulate sales. In 1919 he and his Works Manager rode two of their machines from Birmingham to London at an average speed of 32km/h (20mph), covering a distance of 193km (120 miles). In addition, his daughter Marjorie was often to be seen standing in front of him on the scooter platform in charity processions around the local streets of Willenhall.

One Autoglider distributor in the north of England even organized a scooter race at Harrogate which was won by a lady (on an Autoglider).

Customers and press did not seem to endorse the manufacturer's claims about comfort, however, and made several unkind remarks about the machine. The result was that in 1920 a new Autoglider was introduced. The major change (apart from the fuel tank becoming horizontal rather than vertical) was the introduction of a rear bodywork upon which was mounted a padded seat. In fact, three seated versions were offered for sale, listed logically as the Models B, C and D. The first two were designed to carry parcels in the rear body, whilst the Model D had a more stylish rear with no commercial connotations.

Contemporary publicity material claimed that this Autoglider would take you anywhere, on any road, in any weather, and up any hill, at any speed from 5km/h (3mph) to 64km/h (40mph). This latter speed appears optimistic.

The Motorcycle magazine dated 24 June 1920 described the Autoglider Type D as 'the little aristocrat offering the maximum amount of comfort and reliability for minimum expenditure'. The Autoglider was certainly a serious attempt at producing simple and effective transport and was significant in that it featured the beginnings of enclosed bodywork that was later to be the fundamental of so many scooters.

In 1921 the Union engine was replaced with a Villiers unit again but this last model was short-lived. Interest in scooters was already in serious decline and even well publicized results from the Exeter trial in which an Autoglider covered 580km (362 miles) in 19.5 hours failed to encourage demand. The Autoglider ceased production in 1921 having only sold in modest numbers.

Above: Designer Charles Townsend often used photographs of attractive female models to help generate interest in his Autoglider scooters. Despite much publicity, however, the Autoglider did not sell as well as hoped.

SPECIFICATION: AUTOGLIDER	
YEAR	1921
CUBIC CAPACITY	269cc
BORE	N/A
STROKE	N/A
COMPRESSION RATIO	N/A
POWER	2.75bhp
TOP SPEED	64km/h (40mph)
PRICE UK	£59 7s 0d

Above: The Autoglider Model D had a more stylish rear body and the fuel tank had, by 1921, become a horizontal cylinder between the handlebars.

Above: Right hand controls are choke (air slide), throttle lever and front brake.

19

Above: Unusual side draught carburettor with cylindrical slide barrel.

Brockhouse Corgi

THE BROCKHOUSE Corgi is a civilian scooter that owes its origins to the Normandy Beaches and the Second World War. A small, folding scooter called the Welbike was designed in 1941, built by Excelsior and used by the British Airborne Forces. It could be folded, packed into a container and dropped, by parachute, alongside the troops. Why Welbike? It was designed in a secret establishment near Welwyn and used a 98cc Villiers Spryt motor. This most ingenious design was taken up and modified by Brockhouse to be launched in 1946 as the Corgi. A number of changes had taken place, most notably the replacement of two small pannier tanks just behind the front wheel with a wide, flat tank mounted above the motor. Other modifications were the addition of mudguards, lights and a stand.

The Corgi, when launched in Mark I form, had spoked wheels and retained the folding seat and handlebar arrangement of the Welbike. This, together with its light weight, meant that it could be carried and stored in the smallest of spaces. To unfold and ready the Corgi for use involved no tools and took no more than two minutes.

The original Corgis could not be simpler, they had no gearbox, no kick start and no suspension. Starting the Corgi is simply a matter of sitting on the saddle, walking the machine forward and releasing the clutch lever. From this point on, the single speed unit will take the rider up to 48km/h (30mph) from its 98cc horizontal, two-stroke motor. The motor is very similar to the original Villiers Spryt engine, designed by Excelsior. Like the rest of the Corgi, Brockhouse Engineering made the little single-cylinder unit.

Later Corgis featured further improvements, e.g. disc wheels, a two-speed gearbox, kick starter and, on the Mark IV model, a full apron to provide weather protection. Large numbers of Corgis were sold worldwide, and when Brockhouse acquired a controlling interest in the Indian Motorcycle Company of Springfield, Massachusetts, the Corgi was sold in America as the Papoose.

Simple maybe, but the Corgi is reliable, sturdy and epitomizes many of the qualities that characterize a scooter. It is easy to ride, light in weight, child's play to maintain and inexpensive to run. With the exception of some special promotional Corgis, all Corgis were sold in black with a maroon tank. They even made a commercial box sidecar.

Above: Part of the original sales brochure showing an early Mark I Corgi. The wire wheels were quickly changed to disc type.

Above: Inspiration for the Corgi came from the military Welbike folding scooter.

Like the Mini years later, the Corgi was classless! Users ranged from vicars to sea captains, housewives to company directors. In the immediate post-war years they sold as fast as they could be made. With a saddle height that was adjustable to any size rider and maintenance that any owner could handle, the Corgi was delightfully easy to live with and due to the folding handlebars and seat, not difficult to store.

The final version of the Corgi (the Mark IV) was introduced in late 1953 and continued production until 1956. It featured a sprung front fork, hinged rear mudguard and a tank-fitting luggage grid. Its two-speed gearbox was operated by a footpedal and the very last examples even had a dip switch for the headlamp!

By the mid-1950s, of course, there was an enormous choice of stylish scooters offering better weather protection on the market. In the face of such competition, the Corgi was simply outgrown and became outclassed.

SPECIFICATION: BROCKHOUSE CORGI	
YEAR	1948
CUBIC CAPACITY	98cc
BORE	50mm
STROKE	50mm
COMPRESSION RATIO	6.4 : 1
POWER	2.1bhp @ 3500rpm
TOP SPEED	48km/h (30mph)
PRICE UK	£66 10s 0d

Above: Corgi Mark II with single speed transmission, folded for storage. The drive is disengaged by folding the right hand footpeg.

Lambretta Model A

THE LAMBRETTA Model A first went on sale at the end of 1947. The manufacturers, Innocenti, had been experimenting with the idea of producing a scooter from as early as 1944.

In Italy immediately after the Second World War there was a desperate need for transport. The Model A had a lot to offer. It was economical (57km/litre, 160mpg at a time when petrol was rationed), had a moderate speed of 72km/h (45mph) and was very easy to ride.

The motor is a 123cc direct air-cooled unit (fan cooling was not to come until several years later in the LC). The motor is mounted rigidly in the frame and drives through a three-speed gearbox and bevel gears down a shaft to more bevel gears and a stub axle on which the rear wheel is mounted.

Unlike later Lambrettas that universally adopted the twist-grip hand gear change, the A model has a foot- operated gear change using a rod linkage from the pedal to the motor. This is the only Lambretta Model to have a foot gear change.

The frame is a pressed-steel box section to which the front of the engine is bolted. The whole of the rear of the machine is supported on the engine castings. The seat, fuel tank and rear storage box are mounted on two tubular rails, bolted to the box section spine with the seat clamped above. The

Right: The first (model A) and last (GP200) Italian-made Lambretta models. The A is the only Lambretta to use a foot pedal for gear selection.

leg shields, offering only the most basic protection, are bolted to the centre spine.

The brakes are unusual in construction. The brake shoes are plain cast iron whilst the brake drums are lined with friction material. There is no suspension, this first Lambretta relies on its low pressure balloon tyres to smooth the bumps.

Unlike the Vespa of the same period that was only offered in one colour, the Model A in its one year of production was sold in green, red, beige, blue or grey. Like the Vespa, it offered cheap reliable and economical transport ideally suited to the non-mechanically minded owner. Its construction and design bear no resemblance to the Vespa, but in its own way it fulfilled its functions as successfully. This revolutionary machine, along with the Vespa, mobilised Italy in 1947 and its derivatives from the B onwards did the same for the rest of the world.

SPECIFICATION: LAMBRETTA MODEL A	
YEAR	1948
CUBIC CAPACITY	123cc
BORE	52mm
STROKE	58mm
COMPRESSION RATIO	N/A
POWER	4.3bhp @ 4000rpm
TOP SPEED	70km/h (43mph)
PRICE UK	N/A

Left: This model B established a new 12 hour endurance record covering 1,582 kilometres (983 miles) at Montlhéry in 1950 at an average speed of 132.6km/h (82 mph).

Below: The A has no suspension. It relies on low pressure balloon tyres and a sprung saddle!

Whilst the B looked visually similar, it incorporated numerous modifications, including suspension. The foot gearchange moved to the left hand, and the wheel size went from 17.8cm (7in) to 20.3cm (8in). Innocenti used it to prove that their little machine was the most economical and fastest in the World for its size. A works Model B broke the 12 hour duration record by achieving 1,582 kilometres (983 miles) at an average speed of 132.6km/h (82mph).

In its one year of manufacture 9,000 Model As were sold (none to the UK). They have survived well. There are still a number of fine examples in existence around the world.

Lambretta LC125

Above: LC motor showing rear knuckle suspension and – for the first time – fan cooling around the cylinder..

THE LAMBRETTA LC is an important milestone in Lambretta history. It is the first of their fully enclosed models. Up until this time, all Lambrettas were open-frame scooters.

The LC is an enclosed version of the C model; both were produced from 1950 to 1952 when they were superseded by the D and LD models. 42,500 LCs were produced as compared to over 87,000 of the unenclosed C model. Compared with the earlier A and B models, the C/LC sold like wildfire. To say they were popular would be an understatement. Everyone in Italy seemed to be gripped by scooter mania, and it was the C and LC that started the export boom for Lambretta. Few LCs were

imported into Britain whilst Cs were used to demonstrate the new phenomenon to motorcycle dealers. By the time sales took off in the UK, Lambretta had moved on to the D and LD models.

The Lambretta LC set the body style which was to run until the late 1950s. The frame was totally different to the preceding A and B models. It now used large diameter tubing and set the format for all Lambrettas that have been produced since, with the exceptions of the Cento and Luna ranges. The leg shield and bodywork are all bolted on to the tubular frame and, unlike the Vespa, are non-structural.

The motor is very similar to the Model B although not interchangeable. It is 123cc, fan-cooled and fixed in front of and behind the cylinder barrel rigidly into the frame.

Suspension is an improvement on previous models with trailing link front suspension and a swinging knuckle at the rear. The front suspension was to pioneer the general arrangement for all subsequent Lambrettas although, in the case of the LC/C, the springs are exposed in separate housings in front of and parallel to the front forks. The rear knuckle is controlled by a spring damper unit horizontally mounted beneath the drive shaft casing of the motor.

Due to the considerably higher cost of the enclosed scooter, it sold in much smaller numbers than the C. Even so, both models started seriously to challenge the other dominant manufacturer, Piaggio for market share. Undoubtedly this was

helped by clever marketing by Innocenti. Using the mechanical components from this machine, Lambretta started record-breaking. On 8 August 1951, Romulo Ferri took 53 world records at Montlhéry. Admittedly, his 125cc Lambretta sported a fully streamlined body and supercharging. Nevertheless, the world was unprepared for the fact that a scooter could take the flying start kilometre record at 201km/h (124.9mph). This achievement survived for over 20 years and many other class records including some for 175cc were broken on the same machine. These included the five-mile flying start at 183km/h (113.7mph), the kilometre standing start at 105km/h (65.2mph), and the standing start one mile at 125km/h (77.7mph). The motorcycle world was impressed!

Few LC Lambrettas seem to have survived. Perhaps one reason is its apparent similarity to the LD. An LC can easily be mistaken for its later, and

Above: Romulo Ferri with the works streamlined record breaker at Montlhéry in August 1951. This C/LC based machine took 53 world speed records.

far more common LD successor. It shares almost the same body panels and it is only the front suspension, mainly hidden by the front mudguard, together with a very different motor (only visible when side panels are removed) that distinguishes this rare piece of Lambretta history. Many have been destroyed without people realizing their rarity and classic status.

The original colours were dark green, light brown, sky blue and red. LCs were not sold with two-tone paintwork. This finish was not to become standard until the later LD models.

NSU in Germany bought the rights to make this model under licence, badged as the NSU Lambretta. When their licence expired, further modifications were made and the NSU Prima was born.

Below: Clean lines and superior weather protection of the LC (the first enclosed Lambretta model) set the style and form for the future of Innocenti.

SPECIFICATION: LAMBRETTA LC125	
YEAR	1951
CUBIC CAPACITY	123cc
BORE	52mm
STROKE	58mm
COMPRESSION RATIO	6 : 1
POWER	4.3bhp @ 4200rpm
TOP SPEED	72km/h (45mph)
PRICE UK	£155 13s 6d

Mors Speed

MORS WAS one of the pioneering French car companies founded in 1907; it was one of the branches of the original Mors factory that produced the Speed Scooter.

The construction is unusual consisting of a cast aluminium footboard and leg shield, to which the motor and a pressed steel rear body is attached. The fuel tank is formed inside the leg shield by a second aluminium casting which is welded to it. Thus forming a void which contains the fuel.

The steering consists of a further aluminium casting with tubular steel extensions for the front fork, and adjustable individual handlebars extending from its top surface.

The motor is a single-cylinder, two-stroke, built-in unit with a two-speed gearbox. Gear change is achieved by two heel pedals (one for changing up and one for changing down) with neutral between first and second.

When launched in 1951, the Speed was regarded as very modern in appearance with its faired-in headlamp and sleek lines. In terms of weather protection, it was not as effective as the Vespa of the same period, but every bit as good as the Lambretta. The single saddle is standard issue with a storage compartment located beneath it, whilst the open body work obviates the need for fan cooling.

Behind the saddle there is a flat section of bodywork with luggage ribs to allow parcels to be carried without damaging the paintwork. A pillion seat was an optional extra along with footrests.

Weather protection could be improved by the fitment of a shield at the front of the handlebars which effectively extended the leg shield's coverage almost to the top of the handlebars.

With 20.3cm (8in) interchangeable wheels and weighing only 60kg (132lb), the Speed is suitable for riders of all sizes. It is easy to handle and comfortable, possessing both front and rear suspension. Unfortunately the Speed does not appear to have been exported from its native France despite the fact that it is superbly constructed and delivers a performance on a par with contemporary Vespas and Lambrettas. The only significant omission is the lack of a spare wheel or the means to carry one. This tiny machine does, however, offer a comfortable ride with good suspension, excellent economy and a very flexible motor. It was produced until 1954 when it was replaced by the Mors Paris-Nice a more conventional, totally enclosed scooter.

Below: Clean and simple lines give a timeless elegance to this 1951 French design.

SPECIFICATION: MORS SPEED	
YEAR	1951
CUBIC CAPACITY	115cc
BORE	54mm
STROKE	50mm
COMPRESSION RATIO	6 : 1
POWER	3.8bhp
TOP SPEED	60km/h (37mph)
PRICE UK	N/A

Above: Aluminium castings form the main frame, legshields and front fork with the fuel tank cast into the legshield. The handlebars are adjustable for height and angle.

Right: Telescopic front suspension and swinging arm rear provide Speed riders with a comfortable ride. The gears are changed by two heel pedals.

Douglas Vespa (Rod Model)

THE FIRST Douglas Vespa was announced at the 1949 London Motorcycle Show. This model, subsequently to be nicknamed the 'Rod Model', was a totally British-built version of the original Piaggio Vespa launched in 1946 in Italy.

The model name originated because of a unique set of rods and bell cranks that transmit handlebar twist-grip movement to the gear selector adjacent to the rear wheel. This gear change was dropped on subsequent models in favour of much less expensive twin cable mechanisms.

The Rod Vespa caused a sensation in the UK when announced in its pale metallic-green (the only colour in which it was made). There were a number of modifications to the original Italian design including the relocation of the headlamp from its original position on the front mudguard to the front apron to meet UK regulations.

The frame or chassis consists of steel pressings to form a monocoque complete with leg shields, footboards and steering column. This unit houses a fuel tank under the seat, an engine under a right-hand blister and a storage compartment in a separately attached left-hand blister.

It would be easy to dismiss the Rod Model as just another scooter until you remember that nothing remotely like it had existed before. It was stunningly simple, unusual and very easy to ride. The world bought Vespas in quantities that no two-wheeled transport had ever achieved before.

The design has stood the test of time and is still sold 50 years on, modified of course, but true to the original design concept.

This first Douglas Vespa sold well and with minor improvements a whole series of models followed (G, GL2, 42L2 etc).

The single-cylinder 125cc two-stroke motor was designed specifically for the Vespa. It is extremely compact with a three-speed gearbox mounted in unit and with the rear wheel mounted directly onto the gearbox. This arrangement does mean that the weight of the motor is on the right side of the machine but this offset weight is not a problem, although noticeable when stationary.

Both wheels are quickly detachable from their car-type mountings (four nuts) allowing (for the first time) the machine to carry a spare wheel to eliminate messy puncture repair on the roadside as with conventional motorcycles.

Top speed for the Rod Model is 68km (42mph), adequate in its day although the little unit will sustain 56-64km/h (35-40mph) running indefinitely. What the Vespa lacks in performance, it

Left: The modern Vespa behind is clearly descended from the Rod Model. Only available in metallic green, the Douglas Vespa enjoyed sensational sales success.

makes up for in manoeuvrability. The wide handlebars, low centre of gravity and small dimensions made the Rod Model very nimble.

Vespas attracted people who would never have contemplated buying motorcycles. Perhaps the un-mechanically minded owners felt there was safety in numbers for very soon they formed scooter clubs under whose auspices vast numbers met and enjoyed runs out and competitive gymkhana style events.

Vespas are sturdy and reliable; many have covered vast mileages and demonstrated unusual

Left: The headlamp was moved from the front mudguard (Italian position) to the legshield to meet UK regulations.

achievements. In 1953 a Frenchman, Georges Monneret, actually strapped his Vespa onto a float, attached paddles to the rear wheel, and crossed the English Channel in six hours. One 55-year-old man, recovering from a serious illness, made a pilgrimage to Lourdes with his wife having never ridden a scooter before. They covered over 2,500 kilometres (1,553 miles) and collectively weighed 178kg (28 stone).

Standard equipment on the Rod Model included an electric horn, Smiths speedometer, luggage carrier, comprehensive toolkit, anti-theft steering lock and a luggage hook on the nose of the seat. Accessories included spare wheel, auxiliary petrol tank and a windscreen.

The Rod Model remains simple to maintain and reliable in use. It is slow in modern traffic and could make long journeys tedious. It is pleasurable to ride in town or on short country outings. It is the direct descendant of the original Italian scooter that ushered in the new world of scooters after the Second World War.

SPECIFICATION: DOUGLAS VESPA	
YEAR	1952
CUBIC CAPACITY	124.8cc
BORE	56.5mm
STROKE	49.8mm
COMPRESSION RATIO	6.4 : 1
POWER	4bhp @ 4500rpm
TOP SPEED	68km/h (42mph)
PRICE UK	£127 0s 0d

Left: The compact motor sits under the side blister and creates a weight bias to the right.

Motobécane Motoconfort

FRANCE ADOPTED scootering in a big way in 1950. Long before people in the UK began buying Vespas and Lambrettas, there was a whole range of French scooters to compete with the Italian offerings.

Motobécane had been manufacturing motorcycles for many years and it introduced the Motoconfort in 1951. Whatever the French do, they do it with style and individuality. The Motoconfort is no exception! The rear body is made of cast aluminium, and the fuel tank is cast directly into it.

The motor is an overhead-valve, four-stroke unit of 125cc capacity with a unit construction, three-speed gearbox operated by a rocking pedal gear change on the left footboard.

The final drive is via a totally enclosed chain in a cast aluminium, swinging-arm suspension unit. The front suspension is by leading fork with springs controlling movement at both ends of the scooter.

The Motoconfort's handlebars are almost a work of art. They are chromium plated with sleek and graceful contours, housing a central speedometer and enclosing all the cables. This was a 'design first' on a scooter, even if the chosen arrangement did perpetuate the (in 1951) typically French reverse control levers.

The top speed, 77km/h (48 mph), is on a par with its contemporaries. However, the single-cylinder, four-stroke power unit provides the Motoconfort rider with flexible low-down pulling power that its two stroke competitors just cannot match. Other advantages of this type of motor are very easy starting and a slow, reliable tick-over.

The Motoconfort was not built down to a price as its very high quality engineering and finish testify. The standard specification includes pillion seat, spare wheel, comprehensive tool kit and a tyre inflator.

Perhaps the machine was over-engineered and over-priced because it did not sell in high numbers. It was phased out in 1954 and replaced with the much simpler and cheaper two-stroke Moby Scooter which sold in much greater numbers. The Motoconfort remained essentially a home-market scooter and, apart from some minor styling changes to side panel grilles, ended its production run looking very much as it did at the start.

Unmistakably French in style and character, the Motoconfort has the distinction of introducing uncluttered clean lines and concealed cables (a modern scooter feature) four to five years before any of its competitors.

Inset opposite page: French style at its best. Note the total lack of cables and clean sweep of the handlebars.

Opposite page: The rear body is a complex alloy casting that hides a 125cc four stroke motor. The side panels quickly detach and the main body can also be removed for major work.

Left: Stylish and expensive, the Motoconfort is well engineered. This unrestored example bears testimony to its durability.

SPECIFICATION: MOTOBÉCANE MOTOCONFORT	
YEAR	1954
CUBIC CAPACITY	125cc
BORE	54mm
STROKE	54mm
COMPRESSION RATIO	N/A
POWER	5bhp
TOP SPEED	77km/h (48mph)
UK PRICE	N/A

Rumi Formichino

THE FORMICHINO (Little Ant) caused quite a stir when launched at the Milan Fair in April 1954. Whilst not the first Rumi scooter, the unorthodox use of alloy castings for its body and mudguards, together with its revolutionary styling, guaranteed instant attention.

Individuality of approach is the hallmark of this Rumi scooter. Its 125cc, horizontal, twin-cylinder, two-stroke motor forms the centre section of the chassis and has an extremely distinctive and crisp exhaust note. The engine is amazingly smooth. There is absolutely no vibration at any speed and the temptation is to rev its little heart out up to its maximum power which, on some of the later sporting machines, occurred at 7,200rpm.

For those old enough to remember the English threepenny piece (a twelve-sided coin), a party trick guaranteed to earn the owner a free drink was to place the coin, on edge, on top of the crankcase with the engine running at tick-over. It was then possible to open the throttle wide and close it back to tick-over without the coin moving. No vibration was, or is, evident from the motor of this little machine.

Whilst many scooters of this capacity and year only offered three speeds, the Rumi enjoys a four-speed, rocking pedal gear change and a performance

Right: This early Formichino has a headlamp connected by cable to the steering so that it turns in unison behind a rectangular fixed glass.

that (if it was a car) would certainly put it in the super sports car bracket.

Due to a low centre of gravity and excellent weight distribution, the tiny Rumi offered outstanding handling and roadholding with a top speed that was 16–24km/h (10–15mph) above most 125s of the same period. The Formichino up to 1957 sported a headlamp inside the front nacelle. This was connected to the steering by a cable so that

it turned with it. Later machines gained a fixed headlamp in the same position as part of a cost-cutting exercise to bring the always expensive Rumi nearer to its rivals in price.

It was not all good news. Weather protection, by scooter standards, was poor and an extremely long and careful running-in period was essential for long life and high performance. To assist this, new machines were restricted by a screw, sealed by the dealer, in the top of the carburettor. Any attempt to tamper with the screw, by anyone other than the dealer, invalidated the warranty. Through the first 3,200km (2,000 miles), the dealer would

progressively shorten the screw, thereby allowing gradually wider throttle openings.

The Formichino spawned two high performance versions. These were the outcome of outstanding achievements by works-entered Rumis in the famous French Bol d'Or 24 hour motor cycle races. In 1956, in the Sports Class, a Rumi ridden by Cambis and Ditail, won, at an average speed of 71.35km/h (44.34mph) in spite of some troubles. This was the first of a succession of victories in the Bol d'Or event. In 1957, Rumi took the first two places in the Racing Class competing against machines of up to 175cc. In 1958 a new 125cc Class was created and Rumi achieved the best performance ever by a scooter when Foidelli and Bois covered a distance of 2,095 kilometres (1,302 miles) at an average speed of 87.3km/h (54.25mph). To celebrate this, Rumi produced a production Bol d'Or scooter. Sharing the same mechanical components as the standard model, this new high performance version was fitted with twin 18mm carburettors, larger finned, chrome-lined aluminium barrels, higher compression and bigger ports. The result was a production scooter with a top speed in the order of 120–130km/h (75-80mph) and still only of 125cc capacity. The Bol d'Or was only sold in gold and white, whilst a single carburettor version of it, called the Tipo Sport, was sold in red, ivory or blue. These colours were extended to the Formichino after 1956 (prior to this only Paris grey was available).

Rumi started making motorcycles in 1949 and continued with scooters and motorcycles into the early 1960s. The company still exists in Bergamo, Northern Italy as an engineering foundry.

Motorcycles and scooters were only a small part of its engineering activity and it is said that it was the hobby of the founder. Why did the company cease making these superb machines? It won a massive arms contract and needed all its production capacity to satisfy it. Incidentally, the anchor on the Rumi badge is believed to originate from the midget two-man submarines made by the company during the Second World War.

Rumi scooters were coveted when new and became instant classics. They are appreciated worldwide by enthusiasts and demand unfortunately outstrips supply.

Above: The twin cylinder motor has its origins in the Rumi Motorcycle. Weather protection is minimal!

Left: This Bol d'Or version features twin carburettors, higher compression and a top speed up to 130km/h (80mph).

SPECIFICATION: RUMI FORMICHINO	
YEAR	1956
CUBIC CAPACITY	124cc
BORE	42mm
STROKE	45mm
COMPRESSION RATIO	6.5 : 1
POWER	6.5bhp @ 6500rpm
TOP SPEED	96km/h (60mph)
UK PRICE	£166 19s 10d

Motobécane Moby

THE MOBY was Motobécane's second attempt at capturing a significant part of the scooter market. Well-known as a manufacturer of bicycles and motorcycles, Motobécane's first scooter, the Motoconfort, was just too expensive to challenge the Italian imports.

The Moby scooter was launched in 1954 in a style that closely resembled the successful Lambretta Model C. The Moby has a tubular frame and the early models (up to 1956) offered only minimal weather protection due to leg shields that stopped halfway up the steering column and motorcycle style mudguards.

Later models were to receive full-height leg shields, a fully enclosed front mudguard and two-tone side panels to enclose a motor increased in capacity to 150cc.

The 124cc all-alloy power unit has a chromium-plated barrel and three-speed gearbox in unit. The final drive is by totally enclosed chain

Above: The Moby is only one of an extensive range of machines. Note the increased panelling and two-tone finish of the later Moby model. The higher legshields overcame criticism of poor weather protection on the Moby SV.

SPECIFICATION: MOTOBÉCANE MOBY SV	
YEAR	1956
CUBIC CAPACITY	124cc
BORE	54mm
STROKE	54mm
COMPRESSION RATIO	6.5 : 1
POWER	5bhp @ 4500rpm
TOP SPEED	78km/h (48mph)
PRICE UK	£167 8s 0d

Left; The 'rubber band' front suspension is clearly visible and gives a very comfortable ride. Later models were to gain a totally enclosed fan-cooled motor.

within a cast aluminium oil bath case which forms the pivoting rear suspension arm.

Front springing of the leading-link fork is controlled by Neiman rubber bands (a system favoured by many French vehicles of the period). The 25.4cm (10in) wheels and 'rubber band' suspension ensure that the Moby is stable. It is certainly one of the most comfortable scooters to ride. Its ability to cope with poor road surfaces is exemplary.

Although clearly built down to a price, this scooter was well equipped with front/rear carriers. A spare wheel (cleverly incorporated into the design) housing the number plate/rear light came as standard equipment.

With little excess weight and a stand that could be operated from either side of the machine, the Moby was a popular mount for female scooterists and, unlike its predecessor, enjoyed good sales in its native France as well as moderate success when exported to the United Kingdom.

The fan-cooled, two-stroke motor is a lively performer having no trouble in sustaining 72km/h (45mph) cruising, whilst returning fuel consumption of the order of 35km/litre (100 mpg).

Contemporary road tests praised the handlebar-mounted turning headlamp (most other scooters of the period had apron-mounted fixed or low front-mudguard-mounted units).

When this model was updated in 1957 with more power and two tone bodywork, it established itself as an excellent vice-free scooter in the conventional mould. Riding the Moby is very easy: all controls fall immediately to hand in the conventional pattern of Lambretta and Vespa. The handlebars are wide and the balance/feel of the scooter leaves little to criticize.

By 1958, however, the Moby was, from a styling standpoint, somewhat dated (although technically still more than capable), and sales fell dramatically. Motobécane simply ceased production and concentrated on manufacturing cycles instead.

Above: Front and rear carriers are standard on this simple practical scooter. The style has always been considered austere.

Right: The spare wheel is incorporated into the rear styling and houses the number plate and rear lamp.

Piatti

THE 125cc Piatti scooter was first shown to the public at the Brussels Motorcycle Show in 1952 where it aroused a great deal of interest. This scooter uses a novel cigar-shaped monocoque.

Although it was designed by an Italian called Vincente Piatti, it was never actually made in Italy.

In fact, Belgium and England adopted Vincente's design with only minor differences. The headlamp, originally mounted on the nose of the front mudguard, was moved up onto the front apron. (In its original position it was below the legal height required in several countries, including England.) The petrol filler was relocated behind the legshield from its former position on the top of the front mudguard, and the single seat was replaced with a pedestal-mounted dual seat.

In England, Cyclemaster Limited (later Britax), who made small motors to bolt onto bicycles, launched the Piatti in May 1956 with a number of features specifically designed to attract female customers.

Piatti advertising was targeted at the housewife customer who was deemed (in 1956) to be independent of public transport (though not actually owning her own car) whilst her journeys were clearly confined to shopping and domestic chores. Perhaps this sexist approach was unacceptable even in 1956-59 because sales were poor. The gamble that sufficient women would brave the elements and become riders did not come off! By then, of course, men would not buy a Piatti for themselves as it was clearly not a machine for them. It was a shame because the Piatti was a very simple, easy-to-ride scooter and could (with a little more development) have been very suitable for town commuting.

The whole engine/gearbox unit forms part of the rear suspension by pivoting on an axis point just below the cylinder barrel. A horizontal, undamped coil spring, one end of which is anchored to the top of the crankcase, forms the suspension by operating in tension, and the rear wheel is mounted directly onto the whole engine gearbox assembly.

The seat height is adjustable over a very wide range, making the Piatti suitable for riders of all

Opposite left: The petrol filler has a sealable vent to allow the Piatti to be laid on its side for maintenance without petrol spillage. A pull knob on the steering column lowers the stand.

heights. The stand is very novel and operated by a pull knob at the top of the leg shields, thereby eliminating any scuffs on rider's shoes when attempting to find it. Shopping/luggage space is available above the front mudguard, inside the leg shields and above the rear-mounted spare wheel. With a wind-screen fitted, a further shopping rack is available behind it.

The motor is a horizontal two-stroke single cylinder with a unit construction, three-speed gearbox operated from the left-hand twist grip. 17.8cm (7in) wheels and very wide leg shields prevent fast cornering although the Piatti, with its low weight and centre of gravity, is very easy to handle in traffic. The scooter does not use fan cooling but is reliant on air entering the front mudguard grille, passing over the cylinder (with radial finning) and exiting through a grille on the rear of the body.

For servicing, the Piatti is simply laid on its side. The filler cap has a sealable air vent so that fuel does not leak when tipped over for this purpose. Altogether this was a clever design that might have sold well if the marketing had not failed so woefully.

SPECIFICATION: PIATTI	
YEAR	1956
CUBIC CAPACITY	125cc
BORE	51mm
STROKE	61mm
COMPRESSION RATIO	7.1 : 1
POWER	4.7bhp @ 4750rpm
TOP SPEED	72km/h (45mph)
PRICE UK	£129 11s 7d

Above: The seat is adjustable to suit riders of all heights and cleverly contains a tool box in its base.

Below: Cooling air enters the front mudguard, passes over the horizontal cylinder of the motor and exits at the rear.

Progress Continental

THE PROGRESS started life in Germany as the Strolch. When marketed in the UK by the Progress Supreme Company, it was re-badged as as the Progress. Later British-built (Villiers engined) fibreglass bodied creations by the same company created a need to provide model types. The original imported version became the Continental, whilst British-built scooters gained model names of Briton and Anglian. This large-wheeled heavy weight is typical of 1950s' German engineering. Substantial construction and high quality components created a luxury mount built to last.

Compared with the Italian scooters of the period, the Progress is a giant. Its dimensions are more in keeping with 350cc motorcycles and even the wheel size of 40.6cm (16in) is nearer to motorcycle than scooter.

Many of the components in the Progress were bought in and these included the single-cylinder electric-start, 200cc, fan-cooled power unit and brakes from Sachs.

Starting is achieved by simply opening the left-hand flap in the bodywork, switching on the fuel, pulling the handlebar choke lever and pressing a fascia-mounted switch.

Once running, moving off involves pulling on the left-hand clutch lever followed by a light prod on

Right: The rear body is quickly detachable to give unrestricted access to a 200cc Sachs motor. The large headlamp rotates with the steering within the front cowl.

the left of the twin pedals to engage bottom gear. After setting off, upward changes can be made swiftly and noiselessly by pressing on the right twin pedal. Down changes are accomplished on the left pedal.

The motor (the same as that used in the Messerschmitt three-wheeler) is one of the finest to have been built in the 1950s. It offers a smooth performance down to 24km/h (15mph) in top gear

and this, with a low centre of gravity and light, responsive steering, has the effect of dramatically reducing the rider's impression of the scooter's size and weight once on the move.

Road-holding, when cornering, is more reminiscent of a true race-bred motorcycle, a result of the large rigid tubular frame, hydraulically-damped front/rear suspension and, of course, large wheels.

One peculiar characteristic is that, under heavy braking, the front suspension rises. This is not dangerous but is certainly unusual as most motorcycles and scooters behave in the opposite way.

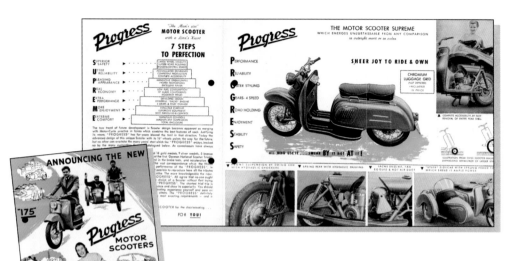

Above: The brochure extols the virtues of the Progress and clearly places it in the luxury scooter market. Major emphasis is placed on the advantages of larger wheels.

SPECIFICATION: PROGRESS CONTINENTAL	
YEAR	1956
CUBIC CAPACITY	191cc
BORE	65mm
STROKE	58mm
COMPRESSION RATIO	6.3 : 1
POWER	10.2bhp @ 5250rpm
TOP SPEED	100km/h (62mph)
UK PRICE	£229 8s 0d

Night driving is facilitated by a 12 volt (big by scooter standards) headlamp that swings with the steering. The large dual seat and carrier (both standard) ensure that long distances can be covered comfortably by rider and passenger, complete with camping gear.

The fuel filler is accessible by raising the nose of the dual seat and, when full, the tank provides a range of 235km (146 miles).

Much of the design is founded on motorcycle practice. However, accessibility of the engine and mechanical components for maintenance is exceptional. By opening the flaps on either side of the rear body, two large clips are exposed. At the side of one of these is a two-pin plug. By unplugging this and lifting the two clips, the whole of the rear body is simply lifted away. From this point on, any maintenance work is as easy to achieve as it is on any naked motorcycle.

The choke lever occupies a space at one end of the handlebars whilst an identical lever at the other operates an automatic neutral selector. At any time, by pulling this lever, the rider can immediately take the scooter out of the gear. A light on the dashboard alerts the driver to the fact that the scooter is in neutral.

The higher cost (it was almost twice the price of several of the Italian scooters of the period) dictated low-volume sales. It may not be a design that one could describe as pretty, but engineering and rideability (assuming the rider is not a lightweight) are of the highest order. Mechanically, the Progress is still practical to run and maintain – thanks to the owners clubs that support the Messerschmitt through spares (new and re-manufactured). Almost every part likely to wear is readily available which makes this machine ideal for high mileage, classic scootering.

39

Above: Neutral gear can be selected automatically by the right handlebar thumb lever and confirmed by a dash light.

TWN Contessa

TWN STANDS for Triumph Werke Nürnberg and was the name used in England to market the Contessa to avoid confusion with Triumph Motor Cycles made in Britain. The Contessa was sold in other parts of Europe as the Triumph Contessa.

From 1907 English Triumphs were made in Germany under licence and still sold as Triumphs.

In 1929 the German Triumph company began to design and build their own distinct range of Triumphs for the domestic market. In the 1950s these were exported to Britain and rebadged as TWN.

The Contessa entered production in 1955 as a high quality luxury scooter offering 12-volt lighting, electric starting and a foot-operated neutral selector.

The motor is a 200cc split single two stroke featuring twin pistons on a common connecting rod in a chromium-lined aluminium cylinder. This unusual technology is designed to overcome the deficiencies inherent in conventional two-strokes of inlet mixture going straight out of the exhaust, when transfer port/exhaust port openings overlap for high performance.

One piston/cylinder becomes the inlet/pumping chamber whilst the other becomes the exhaust chamber. A common combustion chamber is formed above both. By separating the inlet and exhaust in this way 'long' port opening can be achieved with resultant high power. That is the good news. The unfortunate downside is high cost of manufacture and the considerable weight of the reciprocating mass (two pistons and the forked connecting rod). The result of all this complexity is good low-down power linked with a dislike for high revolutions.

SPECIFICATION: TWN CONTESSA	
YEAR	1956
CUBIC CAPACITY	197cc
BORE	45mm
STROKE	62mm
COMPRESSION RATIO	6.5 : 1
POWER	10.4bhp @ 4800rpm
TOP SPEED	97km/h (60mph)
UK PRICE	£230 15s 9d

Left: Two-tone paint (light/dark blue originally) was standard, as was the spare wheel, dual seat and neutral selector. Gear change is by rocking pedal.

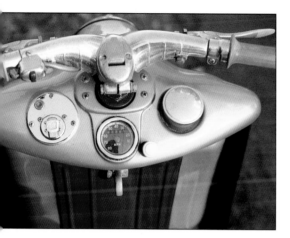

Above: Fuel tanks are mounted in the legshields to assist balance. Two tanks are fitted, one on each side of the steering.

The designers clearly recognized the suitability of the Contessa for sidecar work and built a sidecar mounting onto the frame. The body style was shared with the German Hercules scooter, although the unique engine swings with the rear suspension on the TWN but is fixed on the Hercules.

The TWN is a heavy scooter although the weight is evenly spread. The fuel tanks (there are two) are mounted pannier-style either side of the steering column alongside the two 6-volt batteries (to distribute the weight).

A high standard specification included two-tone paint, spare wheel, neutral selector, front/rear mudflaps lockable tool kit, steering lock and pillion/dual seat.

The quality of engineering matches the high specification/price making a Contessa a reliable scooter to use.

Above: In Germany the TWN badge reads Triumph. It was changed on export scooters so that it was not confused with British Triumph products.

DKR Defiant

THE DKR initials came about because of the business union of a man called Day (who became the MD of DKR), Cyril Kieft (a 1950s racing car maker), and Willenhall Radiators who made the body pressings for this scooter. (The letters DKW could not be used as there was already a scooter manufacturer with this name).

Previously (in 1955) Cyril Kieft had imported and sold the German Hercules scooter rebadged as a Kieft in the UK. He developed a re-engined version of the Kieft in 1956 by replacing the original Sachs 191cc unit with a 197cc Villiers motor. From this, it was but a short step to redesign the front bodywork, change metric to imperial

Above: Two-tone colour schemes are standard on the DKR. The rear body houses a 200cc Villiers 9E motorcycle motor with fan-cooling and electric starting.

Below: According to the sales brochure, the locker lid in the front apron becomes a picnic tray (it has a stay which supports it in the horizontal position). Picnics must have been very small affairs in 1957!

42

sizes for all nuts, bolts and bushes, and – hey presto – enter the DKR Dove (albeit only as a 150cc with kick starting). Perhaps DKR considered the luxury Kieft's high price was its downfall and believed that the considerably downgraded, cheaper Dove was the answer.

This all-British company launched the Dove scooter in 1957. It still retained much from the Hercules scooter. The frame, suspension and rear bodywork are almost identical. The bulbous nose is unique to the DKR range and came about because the triangular fuel tank is mounted ahead of the steering column (just behind the headlight). The shape was controversial, people either loved it or hated it, but few were indifferent to it. In any event, DKR acquired a reputation for excellent handling and solid construction.

It was not long before DKR decided that their chassis could take more power. As the Dove had a Villiers 150cc kickstart motor, it was a simple matter to exploit the engine supplier's ability to provide other capacities. Soon the range was extended to include Pegasus (150cc electric start), Defiant (200cc electric start) and Manx (250cc twin cylinder electric start).

Visually the same, all had foot-pedal, four-speed gear change and 25.4cm (10-inch) wheels, although the tyre size increased from 350 x 10 to 400 x 10 on the larger machines. The Defiant was the best seller (and arguably the best all-round DKR.

Right: The controversial front styling of the Defiant is the result of mounting the triangular fuel tank directly in front of the steering column. This dictated the bulbous nose considered by many to give it its unique character.

The Villiers 9E motor was a successful power plant well suited to the heavy construction. Unit construction, fan cooling and electric starting made the scooter/microcar version of the 197cc motorcycle power unit an excellent choice. Standard specification included a host of bright colours, a sizeable glove box, or storage bin inside the legshield and even a picnic tray (well that's what the brochures of the day called it!), actually it was the lid of the glove box.

Two-tone colour schemes offered were pink/ivory, black/ivory, blue/ivory, maroon/ivory and green/black. Any colour was available to special order (£15 extra).

Although the style was considered by some to be ugly, in it's day the Defiant developed loyal followers who consider it had real character. It is comfortable, easy to live with and offers good weather protection. Love it or hate it, the DKR was, and is, a sound and usable mount. The world was divided about the styling!

SPECIFICATION: DKR DEFIANT	
YEAR	1957
CUBIC CAPACITY	197cc
BORE	59mm
STROKE	72mm
COMPRESSION RATIO	7.25 : 1
POWER	8.4bhp @ 4000rpm
TOP SPEED	97km/h (60mph)
UK PRICE	£188 1s 3d

Maico Mobil

MAICO BEGAN business in Germany as a bicycle maker in 1926. By 1936 the company had started producing motorcycles using ILO engines of up to 143cc in size.

After the Second World War, Maico built a range of single- and twin-cylinder, two-stroke motorcycles under the name of Blizzard. In 1951 the unusual looking Mobil scooter with its fully enclosed bodywork was introduced

The Mobil is unique and owes little to any other machine in terms of its construction and style. Its *raison d' être* is to provide the maximum weather protection and carrying capacity for the rider and/or passenger.

The frame or chassis is a multi-tube space frame made from small-diameter steel tubing. This framework houses a 200cc four-speed, single cylinder, two-stroke motorcycle motor with fan cooling positioned well forward in the frame, such that the rider's legs straddle it. The wheels are large by scooter standards at 35.6cm (14in) supported at the front in a telescopic fork (motorcycle style) and a swinging arm at the rear.

The main body is a composite of steel and aluminium bolted directly to the tubular space frame, whilst the nose section is an aluminium pressing, again bolted to the tubular framework. The rear is styled to form large in-built panniers with a storage area under the pillion seat, and a standard fitting spare wheel is housed within the rear face of the body.

It would be more accurate to say that the rider sits in the Maico Mobil, rather than on it, as the front bodywork wraps around the narrow handlebars so that the integral windshield and front apron totally protect the rider from wind and rain when in motion.

A large semi-circular dashboard in front of the steering column, which is enclosed by the screen, houses the fuel filler, ignition switch and a large speedometer.

The Mobil is a large machine but it is not heavy. The combination of very light space frame and aluminium for the bodywork results in an easy-to-handle scooter, even if ground clearance is a little short for enthusiastic

Left: A car on two wheels (and a luxury car at that!).

cornering. But this is missing the main point. The Maico Mobil was advertised as 'the car on two wheels'. (The Unibus in 1920 made the same claim.) The Maico Mobil is much nearer the concept than the Unibus ever was. Providing the rider does not have to stop, it is possible to ride the Mobil in quite heavy rain without getting wet.

The Mobil's ability to carry luggage combined with its large wheels and effective suspension makes it an excellent touring machine. When new it was expensive and so only for the discerning customer. Today, Mobils are prized possessions and continue to delight their owners. A range of colours, including some two-tones, were available and this highly individualistic machine was considered a design classic when new. Time has not diminished that status.

Above: A small diameter tube space-frame keeps weight low whilst a mid-engine and large wheels provide good balance.

Below: The rider sits 'in' a Mobil with a vast dashboard ahead of narrow handlebars. The fuel filler is on the right and the gear indicator is in the speedometer.

SPECIFICATION: MAICO MOBIL	
YEAR	1957
CUBIC CAPACITY	197cc
BORE	65mm
STROKE	59.5mm
COMPRESSION RATIO	7 : 1
POWER	10.3bhp @ 5350rpm
TOP SPEED	97km/h (60mph)
PRICE UK	£209 11s 8d

Left: The weather protection afforded by the front apron and screen of the Mobil is outstanding. Much of the panel work is in light aluminium making this large machine very easy to handle.

45

NSU Prima D

THE NSU Company is one of the most respected German engineering enterprises with a history going back to 1873. The initials are derived from Neckarsulm, the town where NSU had its base. Originally a manufacturer of mechanical knitting machines, by 1886 NSU were making bicycles. In 1900, the first NSU motorcycle was produced using a Swiss motor.

The Prima evolved from NSU's purchase of a licence to manufacture the Lambretta scooter in 1951. These early machines were named NSU Lambretta and were basically LC Lambrettas incorporating some German components. When the licence expired, NSU continued to produce their own 150cc scooter and renamed it the NSU Prima (later to be designated Prima D to differentiate between this and other Prima models).

The Prima D was first launched at the 39th Brussels Show in January 1956 and, whilst at first glance it appeared similar to the Lambretta LC, was a much improved version with many modifications. The result of all the changes was a luxury scooter made to the highest standards of workmanship.

The engine capacity had grown from the original 125cc to 150cc and gained 12-volt electric starting. The rear suspension featured a new hydraulic shock absorber that greatly improved

Right: A prop stand and main stand were standard equipment along with very comfortable rubber saddles, low fuel warning light and 12-volt electric starting.

handling and comfort, whilst the front suspension had been completely redesigned and more closely followed later Lambretta practice. A very large silencer replaced the earlier Lambretta offerings, and refinements to the gear selection ensured that the three-speed gearbox was delightful to use.

In sum, a utilitarian and adequate Lambretta was converted into a true luxury scooter. Comfort was outstanding on independently sprung rubber saddles, whilst standard specification included a spare wheel, a low fuel warning light in the speedometer and a dashboard-mounted choke lever that was automatically closed when the twist grip accelerator was open.

The bodywork also received subtle modification and extra bright work in the form of anodized, aluminium trim. Vibrant, two-tone paintwork and handlebars that cleverly concealed all the cables ensured a very clean and smart appearance.

These qualities were soon to make the Prima one of the top-selling scooters in Germany. It also enjoyed excellent sales in the UK and other parts of Europe. The Dynastart unit that started the motor

Left: Vivid two-tone colour schemes and an abundance of anodised aluminium trim disguises the Lambretta ancestry of this pair of Prima D's.

Left: The NSU was built for comfort and ease of use rather than high speed.

SPECIFICATION: NSU PRIMA D	
YEAR	1957
CUBIC CAPACITY	147cc
BORE	57mm
STROKE	58mm
COMPRESSION RATIO	6.3 : 1
POWER	6.2bhp @ 5000rpm
TOP SPEED	88km/h (55mph)
PRICE UK	£198 6s 9d

also produced a 12 volt charging system to keep the twin 6-volt batteries, mounted behind the leg shields, fully charged.

The chassis of the scooter is tubular and all of the body panels are bolted on. Unlike the Lambretta it was based on, however, the handlebars are of pressed steel construction.

The high specification also includes a prop stand, centre stand, steering lock, rear carrier and baggage hook. A wide variety of single colour and two-tone options were available. Almost every part can still be sourced from specialist suppliers in Germany.

Unfortunately for the Prima D, NSU brought out a higher powered, 175cc machine towards the end of 1957. This new machine bore little resemblance to the Prima D but its introduction seriously damaged the sales of the earlier model. This was a shame, as the engineering quality of the Prima D is superior, and its general practicality makes it a pleasant machine to own and use.

If the Prima D has a weakness it is perhaps the brakes. Basically they are just too small. They must be maintained in first-class condition in order that the performance of the scooter remains adequate in modern traffic.

One of the outstanding impressions of this machine is the high degree of silencing of both carburettor and exhaust. Even the noises made by this machine are extremely subdued and exude an air of quality.

47

BSA Sunbeam

BSA IS one of Britain's most famous motorcycle makers. Originally an arms manufacturer which explains the origin of the initials (Birmingham Small Arms), they swallowed up several other famous motorcycle manufacturers. By the mid-1950s even this die-hard motorcycle company could not ignore enormous sales being won by Vespa and Lambretta.

The BSA Sunbeam was not their first attempt to move into the scooter market. This occurred in 1955 when the BSA Beeza was exhibited at Earls Court. Despite being one of the stars of the show, BSA decided not to put it into production. BSA had acquired Triumph (its main rival) in 1951 and not

much happened until 1958 when a totally new machine was launched under two names, the BSA Sunbeam and the Triumph Tigress. Identical in construction, these badge-engineered scooters were initially only available in polychromatic green for the Sunbeam and polychromatic pale blue for the Triumph. Two engine sizes were available, a 175cc two-stroke and a 250cc four-stroke twin cylinder.

Unlike many half-hearted scooter creations, the BSA Sunbeam/Triumph Tigress represented a determined bid by Britain's biggest group in the two-wheeled industry to capture a major part of the world scooter market. The 250cc model was also available in two forms, kick start (6-volt) or electric start (12-volt). The BSA Sunbeam/Triumph Tigress in its 250cc form is probably the best British scooter produced. It is quiet, powerful, stylish and good to ride. For the first time, a UK motorcycle manufacturer had designed a power plant specifically intended for the scooter. BSA had not attempted to modify a motorcycle motor and components, but had instead designed the machine as a complete entity.

The BSA Sunbeam has much to commend it. Clever use of single-sided front and rear suspension means that either wheel is quickly detachable and interchangeable. Just three nuts are all that hold either wheel in place, making the optional spare very easy to fit.

Road performance of the 250cc is superior to most standard scooters with a top speed in excess

Left:: Two-tone paint and attractive models were used to promote the sales in the early 1960s. Unfortunately, they were unsuccessful in boosting sales to acceptable levels in the already declining scooter market.

Above: Polychromatic green was the only colour available whilst windscreen, carrier and spare wheel were genuine BSA accessories.

of 113km/h (70mph) and high levels of torque that allow sustained high-speed cruising. In addition, the four-stroke engine gives good fuel economy and easy starting.

The frame is a duplex tubular cradle onto which all the body panels are bolted. Final drive is via a totally enclosed chain and the four-speed gearbox is controlled by a single toe pedal that slides forwards and backwards to change up and down through the ratios.

The front suspension is, in essence, a pair of forks with both legs on the same side of the wheel, the legs being telescopic. The front leg houses a hydraulic damping unit and the rear leg the main suspension spring.

In its original form, the BSA Sunbeam/ Triumph Tigress did demonstrate a couple of design weaknesses. The first was the build-up of heat in the rear body from the exhaust pipes. They ran just inside the body from the engine right to the rear most section of the machine where the silencer was mounted. On later machines the exhaust was redesigned to run down and under the footboards to a silencer immediately behind the front wheel. This reduced the temperatures inside the rear body

and made the machine more pleasant to use in hot weather. The second Achilles' heel was the clutch. Whilst adequate for sensible use, the hard pounding that some riders subjected it to (making full use of the high performance) soon resulted in broken clutches, and a sullied reputation. Despite these minor failings, the BSA Sunbeam offers handling on a par with the best Italian machines with style and performance to match.

Unusually, the only theft prevention measure offered was a steering lock. No key is required to operate the ignition switch and no lock is provided

for the dual seat which covers tools and petrol filler. The disadvantage is that itchy fingers can leave a parked machine with a flat battery, no fuel or missing a tool kit. Perhaps BSA did not believe that street crime was a problem in the late 1950s. A full range of accessories was available, including windscreen, a spare wheel, rear carrier, panniers etc. Access for maintenance is excellent – once 12 bolts are removed the whole rear body comes away in two halves, rather like an Easter egg.

Later machines were offered in two-tone colour schemes of blue and cream or red and cream ,whilst the Triumph versions came in other two-tone colours. A neutral selector was also standard equipment.

In sales terms, the BSA Sunbeam could not be termed a success. Although it sold reasonably well, it did not meet its forecast targets. It soldiered on until 1964. It was not its reliability or suitability that was at fault, basically it was just introduced five years too late!

SPECIFICATION: BSA SUNBEAM B2	
YEAR	1958
CUBIC CAPACITY	249cc
BORE	56mm
STROKE	50.6mm
COMPRESSION RATIO	6.5 : 1
POWER	10bhp @ 5000rpm
TOP SPEED	113km/h (70mph)
PRICE UK	£184 10s 0d

Left: Single-sided suspension makes wheel changing simple and the rear body removes like two halves of an easter egg for servicing. The car uses the same motor.

Dayton Albatross

DAYTON CYCLE Company was a small bicycle maker based in North West London. It was one of the earliest UK manufacturers to create a full-sized scooter.

The first Albatross was launched in 1954 using a conventional Villiers Mark 1H 225cc single-cylinder, two-stroke motor. This choice of motor largely determined many of the much criticised styling decisions which were to limit the early success of what was, essentially, a useful, large-scale touring scooter. In 1954, fan-cooled power units, suitable for enclosure in scooters, were not available from Villiers. In enclosing the motor, Dayton had to ensure that the cylinder received adequate cooling air flow. This resulted in a strange body design and a very small front mudguard. This was chosen in order to allow air to pass around the front wheel, through a tunnel between the rider's feet and then around the cylinder.

Hot air was able to escape from side vents and a main exit just behind the dual seat. The crankcase

Below: The 'Empire' Albatross was created to overcome criticism of the original front fork/mudguard design. The mudguard was also available to upgrade original machines.

Above: A shape born out of necessity. The motor relies on cooling air passing around the small front mudguard.

of this motorcycle power unit was also very wide and protruded through the rear body on both sides (a styling feature which was to persist throughout the life of the Albatross).

The styling of these early machines was considered by many to be cluttered and ungainly. It was a shape, after all, that was determined by function rather than form. Dayton did try to compensate for some of its styling shortcomings by offering a very wide range of colour schemes. When launched, one such colour scheme (lime and black) gained many column inches of publicity in the motoring press (not all complimentary). Despite the styling, the Dayton was eminently practical and gained favourable press for its performance and handling.

Dayton's partnership with Villiers was to continue throughout the life of the Albatross. A new 250cc twin-cylinder (Villiers 2T) power unit was added in 1957. With this motor, the Dayton has

a top speed in excess of 116km/h (72mph), and with its 30cm (12in) wheels, has handling to match.

Dayton's first attempt to improve on the 'controversial' styling of the Albatross resulted in a much larger, stylish front mudguard on a model named the Empire. This cosmetic change was short-lived. In 1958 a totally new, restyled front emerged on the Continental Twin which most testers of the day described as handsome. At long last the Dayton had an appearance that complemented its capability.

The Dayton Albatross Continental Twin is not a run-of-the-mill scooter. It was, and is, a machine for the enthusiast. Much of its design has its roots in motorcycling. It still has ducted air to the non-fan-cooled power unit and its size makes it unsuitable for a lightweight rider. This big machine has narrow motorcycle-like handlebars and is more suited to long-distance, high-speed touring than weaving through heavy traffic. Touring capability is built into the Dayton in the form of a pannier frame mounted on the rear body either side of the rear wheel. A large, dual seat, excellent brakes and a comfortable riding position make the Albatross a good choice for discerning enthusiasts. Of the relatively small number made (albeit over quite a number of years), a fair number survive. They were generally not bought by the casual commuter but by those who really valued their purchase.

Such owners have not just thrown away their scooters. The Dayton was, and is, a little bit special and, with the relative abundance of Villiers parts, is a simple machine for the classic scooterist to use and enjoy. It is still capable of providing pleasurable, modern-day scootering.

Above: The Continental Twin has a much improved frontal style and in this form is a fine long distance tourer.

SPECIFICATION: DAYTON ALBATROSS CONTINENTAL	
YEAR	1958
CUBIC CAPACITY	249cc
BORE	50mm
STROKE	63.5mm
COMPRESSION RATIO	8.2 : 1
POWER	15bhp @ 5500rpm
TOP SPEED	116km/h (72mph)
PRICE UK	£227 4s 7d

Jawa Cezeta

NOT MANY East European scooters were successfully exported to the West. The Jawa Cezeta is an exception. Launched in 1956, the Jawa achieved considerable success in its native Czechoslovakia as well as being manufactured under licence in New Zealand, and exported to Western Europe including the UK and Holland. The style of the Cezeta remained unchanged throughout its production life although mechanically it continued to be refined.

The style of this scooter is most distinctive with its headlamp mounted at the nose of a very long front mudguard surmounted by the fuel tank. The layout provides excellent weight distribution whilst the long wheelbase and large wheels ensure a comfortable and stable performance.

The motor is derived from the CZ175cc motorcycle engine. It is a single-cylinder, two-stroke, air-cooled unit and in all but the earliest model, is fan-cooled.

The frame of the scooter is formed by a monocoque body, made of pressed sheet steel with reinforcement at all high stress points. Front and

Above: English and Dutch brochures show the change of name. The rear view disguises the need (in England) to move the headlamp.

SPECIFICATION: JAWA CEZETA	
YEAR	1958
CUBIC CAPACITY	171.7cc
BORE	58mm
STROKE	65mm
COMPRESSION RATIO	7.4 : 1
POWER	8bhp @ 4750rpm
TOP SPEED	90km/h (56mph)
UK PRICE	£169 19s 6d

Left: The fuel tank above the front wheel ensures good weight distribution. The indicators are standard.

rear suspension is by pivoted fork employing coil springs and oil dampers.

There is a spacious luggage compartment under the dual seat. Whilst many Cezetas have kick starters, electric starting was offered from 1960.

In Holland the Cezeta name was changed to la Bohéme and a whole range of two-tone colour schemes were available.

Standard equipment includes a tool kit, prop and main stands, flashing direction indicators and locks protecting the steering and luggage compartment. In addition, a luggage grid is mounted on top of the fuel tank making the Jawa an excellent touring scooter.

For the UK market, the headlamp height did not meet construction and use regulations. Officially imported machines were therefore modified by moving the headlamp onto the front apron and relocating the horn to the original headlamp position.

This scooter was built to last and is still plentiful in its native Czech Republic. Never a high volume seller in Western Europe, the Cezeta is distinctive and stylish. Some customers were put off by the idea of a fuel tank mounted on the nose, although there are no records to indicate that this caused serious problems and it undoubtedly improved the balance of the machine. Early models had exposed handlebars and were devoid of indicators, whilst later ones were offered with a wide range of extras including a spare wheel, a rear luggage carrier, windscreen and whitewall tyres.

Right: A wide dual seat and long spacious footboards make the Cezeta a comfortable mount.

Maicoletta

The unusual Maico Mobil scooter launched in 1951 has been a considerable success for Maico, and this was followed in 1955 by the large, luxurious Maicoletta. Like the Mobil, the 35.6cm (14in) wheels are large by scooter standards; however, the rest of the machine follows conventional scooter styling. The original Maicoletta had a 175cc motor, although for export purposes a 250cc fan-cooled version of a motorcycle unit was used.

At 146kg (322lb) the Maicoletta is no lightweight. It has hydraulic telescopic forks and rear swinging-arm suspension. In every way the Maicoletta is a long way from the rationale of the lightweight Italians. It is a machine designed for long-distance, high-speed luxury travel and in this respect, it delivers.

The Maicoletta was produced from 1955 to 1962, by which time a 277cc version was included, this latter being specifically targeted at the UK market and for those who wanted to use a sidecar. The 277cc machine is no faster than the 250cc model but has greater hill-climbing ability.

Although officially the top speed claimed for the Maicoletta was 106km/h (66mph), most Maico owners know that it is capable of 113km/h (70mph) even two-up.

The design of this large machine owes more to motorcycle traditions than to scooters. The handlebars are flat and narrow, whilst cornering is accomplished by leaning the machine with little or no steering movement.

The Maicoletta has many excellent qualities and few faults. It is beautifully engineered and finished with many interesting and delightful features. The dashboard consists of two large instruments, an 8-day clock and a speedometer. Within the speedometer is an indicator informing the rider which of the four gears is selected from the rocking-pedal gear change.

A steering damper is fitted as standard, controlled by a large milled ring just under the handlebars. This is a great asset when using a sidecar, although for solo work the handling needs no such assistance.

The dual seat is one of the most comfortable ever fitted to a two-wheel machine and probably also one of the largest. Rider and passenger have plenty of room to readjust position, making long distance travel an absolute pleasure. Comfort is a strong point; however, ground clearance is not. The frame, suspension and wheel size inspire absolute

Below: One bolt releases the whole rear body for easy maintenance. The large wheels inspire real confidence, although poor ground clearance limits fast cornering.

confidence, but the 11cm (4.3in) ground clearance and wide footboards severely hamper enthusiastic riders. The only way to corner a Maicoletta at the high speed it is capable of is to adopt the riding style of a modern motorcycle racer.

Ground clearance is not the only weakness. The 6-volt electric starter is the scooter's worst feature. This dynastart, unlike its 12-volt contemporaries, is designed to rock the engine backwards and forwards against compression until inertia builds up sufficiently to carry the piston over top dead centre, where-upon, hopefully, the engine will start. This rocking motion requires a control box with points to alternate electrical feed creating the washing machine-like action. In practice, if this system is perfectly set up and the battery is in a high state of charge, it will usually work. Unfortunately, anything less than a perfect set-up will achieve a constant rocking (which even sounds like a washing machine) but no start. Unlike the electric start Dürkopp Diana, no kick start is fitted to this machine and it is a very heavy machine to bump start! Just why Maico persisted with the 6-volt starter for so many years is not clear when most other German electric start scooters used successful Bosch/ Norris 12-volt systems.

The Maicoletta has an enthusiastic following and inspires great confidence as a long-distance tourer. Many feats have been accomplished on them. For example, in November 1956 a totally standard Maicoletta travelled from London to Edinburgh at an average speed of 70.4 km/h (43.7mph), and it was clocked at one point on the journey at 125km/h (78mph) by the accompanying large motorcycle.

In the Isle of Man a Maico was run for twenty-four hours around the TT course and covered 1,709 kilometres (1,062 miles) at an average speed of 71.22km/h (44.26mph) despite terrible weather conditions.

A Maicoletta won the 250cc class at the first-ever UK scooter road race at Crystal Palace. Despite production ceasing in 1962, UK importers continued to build and sell new Maicolettas from spare parts bins until 1966.

Reasonable numbers survive and are regarded as true classics. Late models in two-tone silver grey/gun metal with white coach lining have an almost Rolls-Royce appearance. To many enthusiasts there is no better scooter.

SPECIFICATION: MAICOLETTA	
YEAR	1958
CUBIC CAPACITY	247cc
BORE	67mm
STROKE	70mm
COMPRESSION RATIO	7.6 : 1
POWER	14bhp @ 5100rpm
TOP SPEED	106km/h (66mph)
PRICE UK	£237 0s 6d

Above: The view most scooter riders had of a Maicoletta as it sped past. The two-tone finish reinforces the grandiose style and quality of construction.

Right: The optional screen and pannier set invite serious touring. There can be no better scooter for the long distance rider. The indicators are non-standard.

55

Vespa Gran Sport

THE GS 150 is widely regarded as the embodiment of the Vespa concept in its purest form. First introduced in 1955 as the top model in the Vespa range, it quickly established a reputation for outstanding performance and turbine-like smoothness.

Originally designated the VS1, this scooter went through minor changes each year culminating in the VS5, which was produced from 1959 until 1962 when it was replaced by the totally new 160 Gran Sport.

Prior to the Gran Sport introduction, Vespas were regarded as basic transport. This model has curves everywhere and even the dual seat is specifically designed to blend in with the styling of the machine. The wheel size rose from 20.3cm (8in) to 25.4cm (10in), and with a top speed of around 96km/h (60mph) the performance was exceptional for the time. The cornering and general handling are excellent, losing the severe lop-sided feel of earlier models whilst still retaining the same basic design. Some enthusiasts claim that GS 150's roadholding is the best of any Vespa, even when compared with those designed up to 40 years later. The offset motor has little adverse effect once underway, and the smooth powerplant delivers its 8 horsepower at 7500rpm giving very lively acceleration and superb high speed cruising ability.

A twist grip on the left handlebar controls a close ratio four-speed gear-box which for the most part doesn't need the clutch to change.

There is no chassis as the whole body is made out of a set of lightweight pressings which are spot-welded to form the spine, rear body and leg-shields. This simple construction, which uses very few parts, owes much to Piaggio's experience as aircraft manufacturers.

The motor adopts the same basic configuration as its compact predecessors. The end result of all the minor changes that went into making the GS was the creation of a world beating scooter vastly superior to its ancestors or indeed almost any other scooter. Performance and handling have become almost legendary. This is the result of that classic conjunction of design and construction that occurs so very rarely; a unique blend that produces a machine that is much greater than the sum of its individual parts.

Below: Extra fuel can be carried in the spare wheel tank (a genuine Vespa accessory) of this VS4.

The riding position is good and controls are smooth in operation. Everything is where it should be for fast confident riding.

Although produced in volume, this is one scooter that is avidly collected worldwide. Even some fanatical motorcyclists, who would deride all scooters on principle, have been known to make an exception after trying the GS. They concede that this, at least, is a true classic with outstanding abilities.

All models of the GS 150 were only available in silver grey. They quickly became popular and established the benchmark for others to attempt to emulate.

If the Gran Sport has a weakness, it is its willingness to just keep on revving faster and faster until, in uncaring hands, it can destroy itself. Given sensible use, it is very reliable and will deliver very high mileage.

In the 1990s the GS is still a delight to use and more than capable of covering vast distances with ease.

SPECIFICATION: VESPA GS 150 VS4	
YEAR	1958
CUBIC CAPACITY	145.45cc
BORE	57mm
STROKE	57mm
COMPRESSION RATIO	6.7 : 1
POWER	8bhp @ 7500rpm
TOP SPEED	93-100km/h 58-62mph
UK PRICE	£194 17s 1d

Right: Timeless elegance and turbine-like smoothness make the GS150 one of the best scooters of all time.

Dürkopp Diana

THE GERMAN engineering company Dürkopp was founded in 1867. Their products over the years included sewing machines, ball bearings, bicycles, mopeds and, of course, scooters.

The Diana range has always enjoyed an excellent reputation for quality and performance. Originally built with a 175cc engine, a 194cc model evolved with a luxurious specification.

When launched in 1956 the original Dianas had a handlebar-mounted headlamp, individual rubber seats and a heel-operated rear brake. A sports version with a tuned motor was soon added. Power went from 9.4bhp up to 12bhp. On the home market, the 175cc version continued in production, although only the 200cc model was exported.

The basic model remained in production through to the mid-1960s (re-badged as the TS) with only minor revisions. The handlebar-mounted headlamp was moved onto the front apron (most Italians, including Lambretta, by contrast had gone from the apron on to the handlebars), whilst the individual seats gave way to a dual seat. The heel brake was changed to toe-operation and from 1958 Dianas were offered with standard two-tone paintwork.

The Diana Sport remained available in an aggressively finished flame red and retained the handlebar-mounted headlamp. Only a few of the

Above: The brake pedal and rubber saddles indicate an early model Diana. Single-sided suspension eases wheel replacement.

SPECIFICATION: DÜRKOPP DIANA	
YEAR	1960
CUBIC CAPACITY	194cc
BORE	64mm
STROKE	61mm
COMPRESSION RATIO	6.5 : 1
POWER	9.5bhp @ 5500rpm
TOP SPEED	100km/h (62mph)
UK PRICE	£211 1s 11d

Right: Alternative front suspension is by pivoting fork. Wheel removal is more difficult although handling is improved.

very last Diana Sports were manufactured with an apron-mounted headlamp.

The specification is luxurious. All Dianas are equipped with both electric start and kick start (the kick start also doubles as a neutral selector). The fan-cooled, single-cylinder, two-stroke unit has a chromium-lined aluminium barrel and is in unit construction with a four-speed gearbox. The whole motor and rear suspension are mounted on a subframe that is rubber-mounted in the main scooter frame ensuring that all vibration is isolated from the rider. The top speed of a Diana Sport is in excess of 105km/h (65mph) and this can be maintained safely for long periods.

The general fit and finish of the Diana is of the highest quality. As a consequence reasonable numbers of this fine machine have survived. The high price of this scooter ensured that it competed at the luxury end of the market alongside Zündapp, Heinkel and Maico. Many years on, they continue to give excellent and reliable service.

Below: Side panels are retained by a quick release central fastener to reveal a powerful four-speed single-cylinder motor.

Excelsior Monarch

EXCELSIOR, A FAMOUS British motorcycle maker since the early 1900s, was another manufacturer who could not ignore the trend of vast numbers of customers migrating from small motorcycles to scooters. Their first scooter appeared in 1959 when they bought cycle parts and body pressings from DKR, mounted their own Excelsior power unit and re-badged it as the Excelsior Monarch. Two models were sold, both with the single-cylinder, two-stroke Excelsior power unit (one kick start, one electric start). One year later, a totally new Excelsior was launched. This was the Monarch Mark II.

The Monarch Mark II had little in common with its predecessor, other than the same 147cc motor which was again offered with kick start or electric start. The

design had abandoned the steel body in favour of glass fibre, and whilst the front bore an uncanny resemblance to the German Hercules scooter, their rear bodywork was completely different and original in appearance.

The heart of the Monarch is a large diameter single-tube frame with swinging-fork front suspension and single-sided swinging-arm rear. Hydraulic shock absorbers front and rear together with an exceptionally long wheelbase make the Monarch a stable and comfortable tourer although the three-speed gearbox can leave the motor gasping for the right gear ratio at times.

Motorcycle experience had shown Excelsior that the majority of punctures occur in the rear wheel. The single-sided rear suspension makes rear wheel removal extremely simple, whilst the problem of adjusting the chain is taken care of by a telescopic section in the rear arm complete with keyway which ensures that the rear wheel is always aligned correctly.

Engine access for servicing is excellent and is achieved by releasing two wing nuts under the seat, unplugging the rear light wiring and lifting the entire rear body section away.

Left: The long wheelbase gives a comfortable, (if leisurely) ride in this 150cc, 3-speed kick-start model.

Above: A small motor in a big scooter hints at inexpensive travel. Optional rear spats are shown in this brochure along with two-tone paint.

Opposite page: The whole body is in glass fibre. The front bears an uncanny resemblance to the German Hercules and TWN Contessa. The rear styling was all new.

SPECIFICATION: EXCELSIOR MONARCH MARK II	
YEAR	1960
CUBIC CAPACITY	147cc
BORE	55mm
STROKE	62mm
COMPRESSION RATIO	7.3 : 1
POWER	7bhp
TOP SPEED	80km/h (50mph)
UK PRICE	£164 10s 0d

Safe and independent travel at less than a penny a mile!...

The Excelsior New Monarch Mk II SCOOTER

Standard equipment includes a tool kit and pump clipped to the underside of the hinged dual seat which also provides access to the fuel filler and petrol tap.

The gearbox is controlled by a rocking-pedal assembly on the right footboard whilst the rear brake follows British motorcycle practice (it is mounted on the left). This arrangement can cause initial confusion among those brought up on continental scooters and motorcycles.

The electric-start version has an ignition key which affords some protection against theft. The kick-start version omitted any form of ignition switch, simply providing a kill button. As no steering lock or dual seat lock is fitted, there is nothing to prevent anyone from starting and riding away a kick-start Monarch if it is left parked. Just why Excelsior omitted to address this fact in 1960 is not clear. This aside, the Excelsior offers a comfortable, if leisurely, ride with a top speed of 80km/h (50mph).

Colour schemes available were ivory, maroon/ivory, light-green/ivory, blue/ivory, red/primrose, grey/ivory, and blue/grey.

Puch Alpine

AUSTRIAN MOTORCYCLE manufacturer Puch launched its RL model scooter in October 1955. This two-stroke machine had a 121cc, single-cylinder motor with a three-speed gear box and a top speed of 64km/h (40mph). A novel feature of the original machine, which was to carry through to the later Alpine, was a rear bodywork which hinged at its front (like a car bonnet) to expose the whole engine and rear drivetrain.

In June 1956, a 12-volt electric-start version (RLA) was launched. Up until 1959, these two models built a reputation for high quality, economy and reliability. With 30.5cm (12in) wheels and hydraulic shock absorbers front and rear, comfort was of a very high order.

1959 saw a complete body restyle with the launch of the SR Alpine. The engine capacity grew to 150cc and again kick or electric starting was offered.

The Alpine has good roadholding, which stems from the well-engineered suspension, good-sized wheels and low, centrally placed engine.

The three gears are operated from a left-hand twist grip and the single-cylinder two-stroke power unit delivers adequate power to cruise comfortably at 80km/h (50mph).

Starting is simple with either the kick-start or electric-start version. A cover in the left-hand bodywork is opened, the fuel tap is turned on, and the flap closed before operating the external choke knob. In the case of the electric-start model a quick press of the key will stir the motor into life, whilst in the kick-start version the pedal usually achieves the same result fairly effortlessly.

For maintenance purposes the rear body pivots at its front lower edge and is retained in position by two snail cams (one on either side of the rear of the footboards). After release, the whole rear body can be pivoted forward and a stay bar holds it in the upright position. Standard equipment includes a pump mounted inside the leg shields and a full tool kit inside the rear body. Two other flaps (lockable) in the rear body contain tools and batteries as appropriate.

As one would expect from Austria's oldest motorcycle manufacturer (founded 1903), excellent engineering is in evidence throughout. and these later models also offer very colourful, two-tone paintwork (light/dark blue, blue/cream or red/cream). Other improvements include better braking and lighting, whilst rider comfort is taken care of with individual saddles or an optional dual seat.

Although the Alpine sold well for a couple of years, fierce competition from Vespa and Lambretta caused its demise by the mid-1960s.

Below: The rear body hinges at the front lower edge for access to the 150cc power unit. The side flaps give access to the fuel tap and tools.

SPECIFICATION: PUCH ALPINE SR150	
YEAR	1960
CUBIC CAPACITY	147cc
BORE	57mm
STROKE	57mm
COMPRESSION RATIO	6.5 : 1
POWER	6bhp @ 5500rpm
TOP SPEED	93km/h (58mph)
UK PRICE	£159 10s 0d

Above: Two-tone blue or red and cream were the most popular options.

Right: The 121cc RL (A) preceded the SR150 Alpine and earned a reputation for quality and reliability. The handlebars are adjustable on this model.

Velocette Viceroy

VELOCE LIMITED was a British manufacturer of drugs and medicines, founded in the 1860s. It was not until 1904 that the company first became involved in the manufacture of Velocette motorcycles. The early years were not a success.

Between the First and Second World Wars, however, Velocette began to establish a name for excellence. It was somewhat surprising when, after the Second World War, many of the successful motorcycle models were withdrawn in favour of the newly developed LE (a small, water-cooled, horizontal twin favoured by the Police Force). The LE failed to reach its projected levels of sales and cost Velocette dearly. The small, air-cooled Valiant motorcycle and fibreglass-bodied Vogue model that followed fared little better than the LE, and never recouped their considerable development costs.

Above: The promotional material for the Viceroy suggests that this scooter has been created for a sophisticated market.

It was during this period of 'clutching at straws' that scooter development got under way. Initial thoughts centred around a water-cooled scooter developed from the LE, but this was shelved in favour of starting from scratch in order to produce what was hoped to be a truly competitive scooter.

The chief designer, Charles Udall, was in charge of Viceroy development and the new 250cc two-stroke power unit was completed in 1957. It was to be a further three years before the scooter was launched at the end of 1960.

The styling of the Viceroy is unorthodox and many were critical of its dolphin nose. The shape, however, was dictated by the interesting mechanical configuration which, was the outcome of Velocette's obsession with fine handling, smooth running and reliability.

Left: The horizontal twin cylinder unit lies just behind the front wheel with a shaft drive to a rear hub gearbox.

64

Above: The dolphin nose allows cooling air to the cylinders whilst the standard equipment screen keeps the rider dry.

The Velocette is a big scooter offering outstanding weather protection by means of sizeable leg shields and a standard fitting windscreen. Rider comfort is further enhanced by 30.5cm (12in) wheels and long-travel, telescopic front forks. The rear suspension consists of a swinging arm and adjustable spring/damper unit.

The motor is a horizontally opposed, twin-cylinder, air-cooled, two-stroke unit with reed valve induction. This is located across the frame immediately behind the front wheel. The resultant centre of gravity is low and forward, creating a very stable machine. To complete the well balanced mechanical components, the four-speed gearbox is mounted adjacent to the rear wheel hub and connected via a car-type dry-plate clutch and propeller shaft to the motor. Electric starting is provided by a 12-volt unit similar to that used on many cars.

An unusual feature of the motor is that both cylinders fire simultaneously. The result of this is almost vibration-free running for a motor that sounds more like a single-cylinder unit. Power delivery is smooth and allows this big machine to reach a top speed of 113km/h (70mph). The reed valve induction endows the Viceroy with brisk acceleration and, when on the move, Viceroy performance and handling are above criticism.

Unfortunately for Velocette, the Viceroy was a sales failure – a mere 682 units were bought. The cost of development and tooling up for production, which was designed to run into thousands, greatly accelerated the downfall of Velocette.

There is no doubt that the Viceroy is a superb machine in all but styling. What little market existed in 1960 for large-capacity scooters had been fully exploited several years earlier. As it was, the Viceroy was released at a time when that market was dwindling and scooter riders were only interested in fashionable Lambrettas and Vespas.

The Viceroy style may be questionable but its mechanical integrity and fitness for purpose as a long-distance, high-speed cruiser cannot be faulted. Always unusual, there are more survivors than its small original production run would suggest. The pleasure of this machine lies in the riding.

Above: The fuel filler and tank are just behind the steering column binnacle which houses a speedometer and ammeter.

SPECIFICATION: VELOCETTE VICEROY	
YEAR	1960
CUBIC CAPACITY	248cc
BORE	54mm
STROKE	54mm
COMPRESSION RATIO	N/A
POWER	15bhp
TOP SPEED	113km/h (70mph)
PRICE UK	£198 0s 0d

Zündapp Bella

ZÜNDAPP WAS one of the major motorcycle manufacturers in Germany, founded in 1917 and rivalling the mighty BMW for popularity (out-selling them with small capacity machines). The range of motorcycles that they built extended from 50cc through to large capacity flat twins.

Zündapp entered the scooter market in 1953 with the launch of a 150cc model closely resembling the 1952 Italian Parilla scooter in 1953. All subsequent Bella scooters were based on this first model; it was simply refined and updated throughout its long production life which ended in 1963.

The original Bella was a kick-start model. A 200cc option was launched one year later. 1956 saw the introduction of an electric-start 12-volt system and model numbers changed from 150/200 to 151/201 depending on the engine capacity.

History does not tell us what happened to the 152/202 and 153 model numbers as the next revision was known as the 203 model and the final models were the 154 and 204. The numbering does not denote precise cylinder capacity for these remained at 150cc and 200cc.

Only minor changes were made throughout the whole series, although the 204 did receive a redesigned crankcase with a cylinder inclined forwards at 45 degrees to provide better cooling.

Right: From left to right; Bella R204, R201 and R200. The telescopic front forks were standard on the R200. The R201 and R204 have leading link front suspension.

These Bella motors are based on Zündapp motorcycle units and do not have fan-cooling. This demands that cooling air has to pass round the front mudguard, through a tunnel to the motor. This air flow then exits from gills behind the rear seat and slots in the side panels (similar to the Dayton Albatross).

The Bella was always well engineered and the early models in particular make abundant use of aluminium castings for footboards and trim. The motor is virtually unburstable and, given minimal maintenance will seemingly run for ever. The Bella is not a high-speed scooter but it will cruise all day in 200cc form at 93km/h (58mph) even two-up. Rider and passenger comfort is excellent on soft suspension whilst the large (30.5cm/12in) wheels ensure excellent roadholding.

The Zündapp Bella really does not have any weak points in its design. It is easy to live, with and in its final form it was offered in a whole series of bright two-tone colour schemes.

They continue to exist in reasonable numbers because of the relatively high volumes of sales, excellent construction and outstanding reliability of the machine. Bella Clubs can provide almost any spare parts that an owner could ever want.

SPECIFICATION: ZÜNDAPP BELLA R204	
YEAR	1961
CUBIC CAPACITY	197cc
BORE	64mm
STROKE	62mm
COMPRESSION RATIO	6.4 : 1
POWER	12bhp @ 5400rpm
TOP SPEED	93km/h (58mph)
PRICE UK	£199 0s 8d

Right: Bright two-tone paint and extra trim indicate that this model is a Bella R204.

Below: The Bella R201 was still available with teleglide fork as an alternative to the leading link. Electric starting became standard.

Sun Wasp

THE SUN Cycle Company of Birmingham entered the scooter market in 1957 with a lightweight 100cc scooter call the Geni. This scooter had a 98cc Villiers, two-speed, two-stroke motor and a 38.1cm (15 in) spoked wheels. It was not a success and the Wasp, when it arrived in 1959, was more conventional in design. It was pitched heavily at the market dominated by Lambretta and Vespa.

In order to cut costs, Sun had borrowed a basic design shared by Panther (the Princess) and Dayton (the Flamenco). The frame, mechanical components and many of the body panels were shared between the three machines with only minor variations to give each an individual character. The Sun Wasp was the model that was the bridge between the other two, having the frame, front suspension, front mudguard, leg shields, glove boxes, rear body, seat and handlebars from the Dayton with the dashboard, side panels and footboards from the Panther. All three machines shared the same 173cc fan-cooled Villiers engine with either kick-start or Siba electric start.

Surprisingly, all three machines used electrical parts from different manufacturers, the Sun having Miller components, the Dayton, Wipac and the Panther, Lucas.

The Wasp consists of a centre spine frame with leading-link forks and swinging-arm rear suspension. The motor is mounted in the nose of the rear body with the final drive by chain.

The gear change is unusual, consisting of two pedals side by side at the front of the right footboard. Change is effected by pressing one pedal for downward and the other for upward changes of the three-speed gearbox.

Despite a short production run, there are two versions of the Wasp scooter. In 1960 minor trim changes and a new exhaust created the Wasp Mark II. Perhaps the most obvious differences between them were the revised colour schemes. Mark I Wasps were silver grey with red side panels or dark grey with light grey panels. Mark II Wasps gained a whole range of two-tone colour schemes.

Despite the 'parts bin' approach to building a scooter, the Sun is a solid and reliable mount. The Villiers engine provides adequate cruising at up to 80km/h (50mph) and well suspended front and rear wheels provide safe handling.

A clever feature is the cut-away sides to the footboards which, – in conjunction with a seat height of only 72cm (28.5in) – makes the Wasp a practical proposition for the shorter rider. One feature of the design that is a disappointment is the horn. For some reason Sun decided to mount this

Left: Cut away footboards enable shorter riders to put their feet on the ground with ease.

on the nose of the rear body. The result is that it is very effective at frightening the rider but little use in alerting someone of the scooter's approach.

The leg shield contains two glove boxes and the fuel tank/petrol tap is located by lifting the standard equipment dual seat. The glove boxes and dual seat are not lockable; perhaps theft was not a problem in 1960!

Despite these minor shortcomings, the Wasp is a stylish and sound design. Unfortunately, it had

to survive in a confusing and over-populated market and so never sold in the quantities that Sun hoped for. It just could not compete with Lambrettas and Vespas, especially on price. The Villiers power unit is dependable and spares continue to be available, which makes making the Sun a practical proposition for regular use today.

Below: The Wasp is a competent design despite the use of many proprietary parts. The horn is unusually positioned.

SPECIFICATION: SUN WASP	
YEAR	1962
CUBIC CAPACITY	173cc
BORE	59mm
STROKE	63.5mm
COMPRESSION RATIO	7.4 : 1
POWER	7.6bhp @ 5000rpm
TOP SPEED	80km/h (50mph)
PRICE UK	£182 14s 11d

69

Lambretta TV175 Series 3

THE BULK of Lambretta sales were based on the company's unswerving loyalty to the original concepts of the scooter, i.e. that it should provide small, lightweight, economical transport suited to the non-mechanically minded.

In addition to this volume market, however, there was a clear demand for higher performance, a fact ably demonstrated and satisfied by machines like the Vespa GS150 from 1955.

Lambretta was already producing excellent 150cc machines, but these just could not compete with higher performance Vespas. In 1957 Lambretta launched its first TV175 with an engine capacity of 170cc and a totally new design. The new TV175 was to set the trend for all full-size future Lambrettas, but it proved, mechanically, to be ill-developed. It remained in production for only one year before being replaced by a visually similar, but mechanically much changed, LI 150cc model. In 1959 a larger capacity LI was launched as the new TV175. This time it actually sported a 175cc motor. This second series TV175 had a very successful production run from 1959 to 1962. It featured, for the first time, a headlamp mounted on the handlebars.

The Series 3 (slim style) 175 was launched in 1962 and this was planned to be the top performance Lambretta (at least for its Italian home market).

By this time, particularly in the UK, the quest for power was on. UK scootering had developed a large competitive element and scooter tuning/high performance versions were big business. Against this background and under pressure from the UK Lambretta concessionaires, parent company Innocenti (with some reluctance), was persuaded to make a 200cc version. The 200 was designated the Lambretta GT and sold specifically into the UK. It was, effectively, a larger bore version of the TV175. The TV175 Series 3 is, in the eyes of many, the pinnacle of Lambretta achievement. It may not be as fast as the GT or later GPs but it has a balance of reliability, smoothness, performance and handling that many enthusiasts would argue has never been bettered by any Lambretta before or since.

The TV175 is clearly a development from the LI 150 slim style (launched at the same time), sporting a considerable number of minor changes. The front mudguard is sleeker with crisper styling, the headlamp gains seven facets on its essentially circular form and a dual seat becomes a standard fitting replacing the individual saddles of its smaller capacity sister.

Below: The seven facet headlamp and sleeker front mudguard (in side panel colour) distinguish a TV 175 from its LI 125 and 150 stable-mates, along with a dual seat.

The real changes, however, are more than cosmetic. The larger capacity motor and well-selected gear ratios deliver a top speed of 106km/h (66mph), enough to compete with the Vespa GS.

To cope with this higher performance, the front forks are equipped with telescopic dampers and, perhaps more importantly, for the first time on any two-wheeler anywhere in the World, a disc front brake is standard equipment.

In the UK at least, the two-tone colour schemes were subtly altered further to distinguish the TV175 from the LI models. LI dual-toning was restricted to the horn casting and side panels, whereas the TV175 includes the front mudguard in the second colour.

The TV175 quickly established a loyal following and remains an excellent vice-free scooter. Ground clearance, weight distribution, handling, steering and brakes are all of the highest order. Unlike its larger/later 200cc cousins, it does not suffer from vibration.

If the Vespa GS combines all that is best in its manufacturer's design concepts, then the TV175 achieves the same for Lambretta.

Pre-dating motorcycles by several years, the provision of a front disc brake was a marketing coup. Many column inches of press coverage were devoted to this feature. World-wide sales amounted to 37,000 compared with more than a million Series 3 LIs. This figure demonstrates that this is a special scooter satisfying a special need!

Right: The first two wheel machine to have a disc brake which is indicated by the vents in the hub.

Below: The slim body style greatly improves enthusiastic cornering and this ability is reinforced by the (standard fit) hydraulic dampers of the front suspension (only on the TV 175).

SPECIFICATION: LAMBRETTA TV175 SERIES	
YEAR	1963
CUBIC CAPACITY	175cc
BORE	62mm
STROKE	58mm
COMPRESSION RATIO	8 : 1
POWER	8.75bhp @ 5300rpm
TOP SPEED	106km/h (66mph)
PRICE UK	£189 17s 6d

71

Heinkel Tourist

THE GERMAN Heinkel company made aeroplanes before and during the second World War. In 1952, unable to continue aircraft production, they began producing high quality mopeds and scooters.

The Heinkel Tourist has established for itself a special following among scooter owners. The magic words that make the Tourist so attractive to its devotees are 'four-stroke'. Powered by a 174cc overhead-valve, single-cylinder, fan-cooled motor, the Heinkel is truly a luxury touring mount. It is quiet, powerful and extremely well engineered. A tubular, rigid frame supports steel body panels and cast aluminium footboards, while the motor is mounted in rubber

bushes to eliminate vibration. The exhaust note is quiet and the hydraulically-damped suspension front and rear provides high comfort and effortless travel over long distances.

Heinkel (AO) scooters were first sold in the United Kingdom as Excelsior Heinkels. Excelsior was a famous motorcycle manufacturer that imported the machines and simply badged them as its own. As the Heinkel was also sold throughout Europe under its own name, this badging was quickly dropped. By the time the second series was introduced with streamlined handlebars and totally enclosed cables, all the machines were simply known as Heinkel Tourists. The second model was known as the A1.

For touring purposes, the Heinkel Tourist was hard to beat as it offered four luggage areas for two-up travel. Above the headlamp was a fold-down luggage carrier, plus a baggage hook inside the legshields, a storage bin under the seat and a carrier on the rear-mounted spare wheel. Camping gear and clothes could all be easily accommodated.

Despite its apparent bulk, the Heinkel is a comfortable and easy

Above: Designed as a comfortable long-distance tourer, the Heinkel enjoyed considerable sporting success winning the first UK Scooter Race at Crystal Palace.

machine to ride. It has a low centre of gravity and good balance. The brakes are excellent and, of course, supplemented by the additional braking that only a four-stroke engine can provide. This last model (A2) gained restyled bodywork, flashing indicators front and rear and a slight power increase from 9.2bhp to 9.5bhp.

The thoroughbred Heinkel was a machine for the enthusiast and many of its buyers entered the world of scooter competition. Heinkels competed in 108 international and national sports meetings between 1958 and 1960, often against heavy competition from motorcycles. In this time they achieved 349 gold medals, 67 gold team awards, 101 silver medals and 62 bronze medals. The first, all scooter race held at Crystal Palace in the United Kingdom was also won by a Heinkel.

The Tourist is an outstanding scooter in all respects. Weather protection is second to none. In fact, one contemporary road tester claimed that only a car could provide better protection. Starting

Left: Colourful Heinkel brochure focuses on sunny-day touring to promote sales.

SPECIFICATION: HEINKEL TOURIST A2	
YEAR	1965
CUBIC CAPACITY	174cc
BORE	60mm
STROKE	61.5mm
COMPRESSION RATIO	7.4 : 1
POWER	9.5bhp @ 5750rpm
TOP SPEED	96km/h (60mph)
UK PRICE	£239 8s 0d

Right: The Excelsior Heinkel (AO) has open tubular handlebars and a more compact rear body than the later A2. Equipment for the Excelsior was comprehensive and included an 8-day clock in the dash board.

73

is electric and usually instantaneous — simply pressing a key is all that is required. Several other aids to better scootering deserve mention: a steering lock secures the front forks on either full right or full left turn, the same key serves to lock the dual seat platform and, if your are a bit careless when parking, an alloy bumper protects the front bodywork. The centre stand is one of the easiest to operate and even a headlight flasher switch is incorporated on the handlebars. On all but the earliest machines, attractive two-tone colour schemes were available. If the Heinkel were a car, it would truly be deserving of executive status.

Left The Tourist in A2 form has direction indicators, front/rear carriers, spare wheel and elegant trim. There can be few scooters that offer comparable comfort and luxury.

Vespa Supersprint 90

NORMALLY REFERRED to as the Vespa 90SS, this is the 1966 high performance version of the well established Vespa 90. It was designed to appeal to the sporting/competitive scooter enthusiast.

The changes from the specification of the standard 90 are numerous. The leg shields on the frame are considerably narrower. The handlebars are dramatically reduced in width and feature an enlarged headlight/speedometer. The engine has its origins in the standard 90 but with larger ports, carburettor and a special sports exhaust. The compression ratio is raised and the increased power is delivered through four gears rather than the three fitted in standard 90s.

The 90SS remains true to the original Vespa design concept even if it has become very slim. The motor still sits at the side of the rear wheel with the very compact gearbox almost inside it. The spare wheel mounted under the dummy tank is standard whilst the space inside it contains a cylindrical storage box. Now highly prized by collectors, the Supersprint

Below: The legshields and handlebars are much narrower than the standard Vespa 90 whilst the dummy fuel tank caused the rules for defining a scooter to be re-written. The standard spare wheel has a cylindrical tool box in the centre.

90 does not survive in sufficient numbers to meet demand. When they do appear on the market, they are usually eagerly and speedily bought!

As it is so light, the performance is outstanding. Acceleration matches that of many 200cc mounts, whilst top speed is on a par with contemporary 150cc scooters. The 90SS became the machine to be seen on in all forms of scooter sport. It was so successful that some people wanted it banned from scooter competitions, arguing that it was no longer a scooter because of its dummy fuel tank mounted

Above: The white SS90 featured in this brochure was not available in the UK. Red or blue was the only choice although this did not inhibit sales.

between the seat front and the headstock. This controversy was responsible for the rules defining a scooter (for the purpose of racing) being changed. Prior to the 90SS, the rules stated that there must be an open space between the seat and the headstock. These were eventually amended after much argument to read that there should be no structural member between the seat and headstock! This rule change allowed the dummy tank (actually a glove box) to remain in place. In fact, its removal made the 90SS like any other scooter and imposed no penalty on performance so it was considered illogical to ban it. Nobody could deny that the lightweight, narrow profile and dummy tank makes possible enthusiastic riding with an agility that a standard 90 and most other scooters cannot match.

Most 90SSs were used extensively in competition which sadly resulted in the eventual destruction of many. Only available in red or blue, the Sprint was regarded as a classic almost from the day it was launched. And so it remains.

Right: Performance lives up to the image with tuned four-speed motor, sports silencer and nimble road manner.

SPECIFICATION: VESPA SUPERSPRINT 90	
YEAR	1966
CUBIC CAPACITY	88.5cc
BORE	47mm
STROKE	51mm
COMPRESSION RATIO	8.7 : 1
POWER	6bhp @ 6000rpm
TOP SPEED	93km/h (57.8mph)
UK PRICE	£133 14s 3d

Lambretta GP200

BY THE late 1960s Lambretta had overcome its reluctance to build large capacity scooters. Sales demand had proved overwhelmingly that a new performance machine was needed.

The 200DL was produced between 1969 and 1971 as the largest and last of Innocenti's famous Lambretta line. In the UK, this model was badged as the Grand Prix 200 and gained a number of refinements over the earlier GT200. Cosmetic changes include a rectangular headlamp, redesigned handlebar cowls, new side panels and black trim in place of the grey of its ancestors.

Late-model motors have electronic ignition and a power boost to 11.9bhp at 6200rpm. With a top speed of 113km/h (70mph) the 200DL is an accomplished performer. Most of the problems of earlier 200 Lambrettas were eliminated by the time it entered production and a properly assembled Grand Prix 200 will reliably cover long distances at high speed.

Although only 9,300 were produced, spare parts availability and interchangability with far more prolific smaller capacity Lambrettas ensure that running a Grand Prix (DL) Lambretta is straightforward and relatively inexpensive. Unfortunately, finding a good example is becoming increasingly difficult as many fell into the hands of owners who regrettably were prepared to push the machine to its limits and beyond.

The colours available for GPs closely match those of the Luna range with vivid orange, yellow ochre, bright red and turquoise all proving very popular. Matt black trim and decals were used in preference to badges, setting a fashion that was to be widely copied throughout the 1970s. Just as the TV175 Series 3 is regarded as the best all-rounder, the DL/GP200 is considered to be the best and most reliable high performance Lambretta. It is not as smooth as the 175, but with a 36 per cent power increase, its ability to sustain high speeds up severe gradients is unchallenged by any other standard production Lambretta and, for that matter, by most other makes of scooter.

When Innocenti finally stopped production of this machine, enthusiasts worldwide mourned its passing. This scooter formed the base for Indian and Spanish licence-built copies, but they seemed never to match the original for quality, finish or reliability.

Left: The Italian Lambretta in its final 200cc form is a handsome and desirable mount with a high performance.

Above: Black trim and decals with a rectangular headlamp identify the GP200 (DL200) as a top of the range Lambretta.

Right: The rear view that most other scooterists had of the GP200 as it passed them. Rear carriers were an accessory.

SPECIFICATION: LAMBRETTA GRAND PRIX 200	
YEAR	1969
CUBIC CAPACITY	198cc
BORE	66mm
STROKE	58mm
COMPRESSION RATIO	7.3 : 1
POWER	11.9bhp @ 6200rpm
TOP SPEED	113km/h (70mph)
UK PRICE	£243 10s 0d

Lambretta Vega

THE LAMBRETTA Vega was one of a range of lightweight, space-age scooters that formed the Luna range.

In Italy, Luna means moon whilst Vega translates into brightest star. Two other models completed the range. These were the Cometa (comet) and the Lui (the small moon).

The Vega and Cometa were 75cc machines whilst the Lui was 50cc. For the most part the Lui remained a home-market product whilst the two 75cc models were exported worldwide.

Styled by Bertone, the famous Italian automotive designer, the Luna range was very different from conventional scooters of the day. Lambretta returned to the open framed look of earlier

Above: Space-age style presented by space-suited girls. The colours were as 'way out' as the scooters.

models. However, despite tremendous publicity with moonscape backgrounds and pretty girls aplenty, initial sales were disappointing. The design was just too different initially for many customers! Once people became used to the radical style though, the Vega began to sell and soon supply could not keep up with demand.

The Vega (badged as the 75s) was the most popular and despite its diminutive size was capable of 84km/h (52mph). The Cometa is essentially the same machine with a unique automatic oil injection system which means that the rider does not need to add oil to the petrol. The main fuel tank is split into separate fuel and oil tanks. A throttle-linked pump delivers metered oil into the engine automatically.

Left: High handlebars and a narrow light-weight 'open' frame gives the Vega outstanding manoeuvrability.

The Vega sports 25.4cm (10in) wheels, four gears and was available in five standard colours — red, turquoise, lime green, yellow ochre and orange. The motor evolved from the Cento range (100–125cc), although even the crankcase castings were remodelled to reflect the new angular style of the range.

Like the Sporting Vespa 90SS, the Vega was soon adopted by club riders for use in competition. The high, wide handlebars, and light, narrow profile, coupled with high ground clearance, made it a winner in gymkhanas and other club sport. The standard 75cc motor delivers a performance that belies its small capacity. Power is nearer to many 125cc machines of just a few years earlier.

The Vega was 20 years ahead of its time when launched in 1968. It had a short production life of only two years but even today will provide very acceptable performance that still gives the latest light scooter offerings a run for their money.

SPECIFICATION: LAMBRETTA VEGA	
YEAR	1970
CUBIC CAPACITY	75cc
BORE	46.4mm
STROKE	44mm
COMPRESSION RATIO	9.3 : 1
POWER	5.2bhp @ 6000rpm
TOP SPEED	84km/h (52mph)
UK PRICE	£130

Left: The Vega sold around the world as this Australian model shows. The excellent ground clearance and high exhaust made the Vega very popular in off-road competitions.

Index